U.S. 40

A Roadscape

of the

American

Experience

US 40

A Roadscape of the American Experience

by

Thomas J. Schlereth

Indianapolis
Indiana Historical Society
1985

© 1984 Thomas J. Schlereth
© 1985 Indiana Historical Society

CONTENTS

Preface: Doing American History on the Road vii

I   Reading the Road: The Above-Ground Archaeology
of the American Highway 1

II   A Road Guide to U.S. 40 in Indiana, Past and Present. 61

III   The Road in American Life—Selected Sources 145

Preface: Doing American History on the Road

This book, like the highway it explores, is many things simultaneously. It is a brief history of American road transportation, a primer for investigating the past and present of the contemporary landscape, a portfolio of documentary photography from the nineteenth and twentieth centuries, and a personal assessment of the cultural role that the road has played in the American experience. Focused on the historical development and physical environment of the route traversed by present-day U.S. 40 across Indiana, this field guide is designed to help its readers see the American highway as a mammoth outdoor museum of American history.

Patterned, in part, after the early auto touring guides of the 1920s, the book is divided into three sections. Part I, "Reading the Road: The Above-Ground Archaeology of the American Highway," is a short primer showing the reader how anyone can identify and interpret the extant physical evidence of the American road and roadside in a way that reveals much of its historical development and contemporary meaning. In the second section, titled "A Road Guide to U.S. 40 in Indiana, Past and Present," the general techniques of the above-ground archaeology approach are applied to the specific Indiana landscape of U.S. 40 over four historical periods: its National Road era (1827-1849); the period of its private highway associations (1850-1925); its resurgence as a part of the national numbered highway system (1925-present); and its role since the advent of the Interstate era (1960-present). Part II also suggests how U.S. 40 has had a major impact on the people of Indiana, past and present, in several aspects of their everyday life; for example, the role of the highway in shaping and reshaping the natural environment, in determining settlement patterns, in prompting new forms of work and play, and as an important civic space. Part III, "The Road in American Life—Selected Sources," is a brief bibliography of resources that I have consulted in my research. I include them both to record my intellectual debts and to suggest studies that might prove helpful to others interested in doing history on the road.

In short, Parts I and II provide new ways of looking at roads as we encounter them in our daily experience. Part I considers the road in general as a *physical artifact*; Part II explores a specific road as an outdoor *museum exhibit*; and Part III evaluates the American roadscape as an opportunity for *cultural research*.

Although the specific road investigated in this volume has had numerous identities and many other names, I will usually refer to it as the U.S. 40 route. I do so for several reasons. To begin with, U.S. 40 is the label that one finds most frequently used on contemporary maps and markers that trace this road's passage through Indiana. Second, it is the twentieth-century cultural history of the road, initiated by designation of it as "U.S. 40" by the Joint Board of

State and Federal Highway officials in 1925, that receives the most attention in this book rather than its life, say, as the National Road in the nineteenth century or as a part of the Interstate System in our own time. Third, I view this modest volume as a contemporary attempt, albeit on a much more local scale, to continue the pioneering work of landscape historian George R. Stewart who, in his classic work, *U.S. 40: Cross Section of the United States of America* (1953), saw this road as "the richest historically of any of the transcontinental highways in the nation." Published thirty years after Stewart's study of the American highway, I hope that this essay will be another contribution to our understanding of the cultural significance of both a particular road, U.S. 40, and also the American road in our individual and collective experience.

While I write here in the first person and recognize that I must take full responsibility for the text that follows, drafting this essay has been a highly collaborative effort. Seldon Bradley, a documentary photographer and the project director of an Indiana Committee for the Humanities research grant that helped support part of the research and preparation of my work, helped me throughout the summer of 1982. We tried to unite the perspectives of the documentary photographer and cultural historian in an interpretation of U.S. 40 that we hoped would help others understand that roadscape with a similar dual angle of vision.

Joyce Bradley, a businesswoman, wife, mother, and excellent cook, always extended me the gracious hospitality of her home and table no matter how late her husband and I returned from our fieldwork on U.S. 40. Equally patient and helpful have been my two typists, Sandy Tengblad and Debbie Condon, two valiant members of the University of Notre Dame Stenographic Service who have typed and retyped the narrative that follows.

The staff at the Indiana Historical Society have also been of immense assistance in supporting, researching, and publishing this study. Gayle Thornbrough, the Society's former executive secretary, has given the book institutional and editorial support from its earliest stages, as has Robert K. O'Neill, director of the Society's library. Of particular help in my archival research have been Timothy Peterson, curator of the Society's photographic collections, and Robert M. Taylor, a historian working on the Society's new guide to the state of Indiana.

A special note of thanks is due the Indiana Committee for the Humanities, who partially funded my research and writing on this project. In addition to the committee members who awarded support to the grant proposal, a personal note of gratitude is due Donna Bucove, associate director of the ICH, who believed in the idea from the beginning.

The numerous intellectual debts that every scholar accumulates in the course of a long research project probably can never be adequately acknowledged. Where I have learned from the published work of others, I have endeavored to designate those titles most useful to me in the bibliographical essay which comprises Part III of this book. I would, however, also like to pay tribute to several individuals who have taught me much beyond their published scholarship. In this context, I am especially grateful to the following persons for their willingness to read my entire manuscript and to offer me valuable criticism: Grady Clay, editor, *Landscape Architecture*; John Jakle, Department of Geography, University of Illinois—Champaign-Urbana; Peirce Lewis, Department of Geography, The Pennsylvania State University, University Park; Wendy Clauson Schlereth, University Archivist, University of Notre Dame; Thomas R. Vale and Geraldine R. Vale, Department of Geography, University of Wisconsin, Madison; and Wilbur Zelinsky, Department of Geography, The Pennsylvania State University, University Park.

THOMAS J. SCHLERETH

I Reading the Road: The Above-Ground Archaeology of the American Highway

In an 1846 Thanksgiving Day sermon delivered at the North Church in Hartford, Connecticut, Horace Bushnell gave a now famous discourse on "The Day of Roads," later published in a book of his essays titled *Work and Play* (1864). In his address, the American minister and essayist made an extraordinary claim: "The road is that physical sign or symbol by which you best understand any age or people . . . for the road is a creation of man and a type of civilized society." The New England clergyman grasped an important insight in recognizing that the road could be viewed as a cultural artifact, a physical entity both reflecting and affecting human behavior. He acknowledged that American history had been, in part, shaped by American roads. In turn, the American character, particularly our fascination with movement, migration, and mobility, had shaped our roads.

Bushnell also realized that much of the evidence for understanding this relationship of people and roads was to be found out *on* the road itself. "You may learn something by going into universities and libraries," he told his nineteenth-century audience, "but quite as much by looking at the road." Bushnell was aware that artifacts such as road surfaces, roadside structures, even road names, contained clues to a nation's cultural history.

Almost a century later another American social commentator, George R. Stewart, a Californian and a professor of literature, took a similar approach to deciphering the American experience from the surviving physical features of the American road. In writing *U.S. 40, Cross Section of the United States of America* (1953), Stewart suggested that we should think of that highway not only as a way of getting from one place to another, but also as an outdoor museum containing a story that could only be told by looking beyond the route lines on maps and the numbers on signposts. To Stewart, the road

> must be not only what can be seen, but also what can be felt and heard and smelled. We must concern ourselves with the land that lies beside it and the clouds that float above it and the streams that flow beneath its bridges. We must remember the people who pass along it, and those others who passed that way in former years. We can forget neither the ancient trees that shadow it, nor the roadside weeds that grow upon its shoulders. We must not reject the wires that parallel it, or the billboards that flaunt themselves along its margins. We must accept the slums of "Truck Route" as well as the skyscrapers of "City Route," and the fine churches and houses on an "Alternate Route." . . . Only by considering it all, as we drive from the east or from the west, shall we come to know in cross section, the United States of America.

Bushnell and Stewart were advocates of what some of us now call "above-ground archaeology"—an

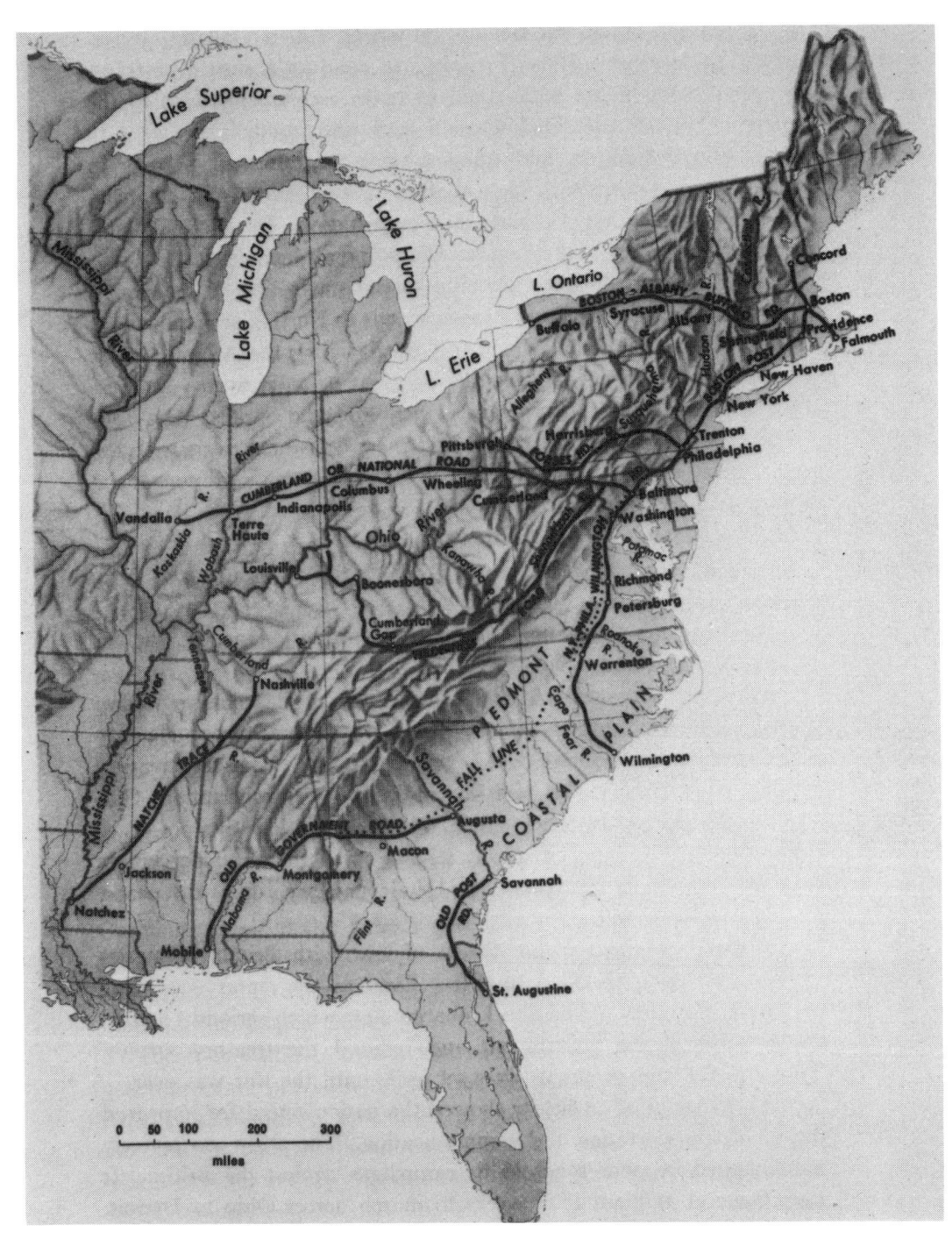

Colonial and Early American Roads. *Rand McNally and Company.*

approach that uses the contemporary environment to help a typical traveler "read" American history from surviving artifacts or material culture of that environment. In short, above-ground archaeology is a simple way of probing, identifying, and interpreting a landscape's extant artifacts, be they bridges or billboards, motels or motorways, in order to gain an increased awareness and understanding of life as lived in the past and present.

Such a definition of above-ground archaeology differs in only one significant way from James Deetz's description of his discipline in his *Invitation to Archaeology* (1967), where archaeology is seen as the work of researchers "who usually excavate the material remains of past cultures and through the study of such evidence, attempt to re-create the history of man from his earliest past and to determine the nature of cultural systems at different times and places around the world." Above-ground archaeologists, unlike their below-ground colleagues, "dig" into the past but usually on the surface; they examine what they find where they find it before it is buried by time and chance. Above-ground archaeologists work with the history still on the land as opposed to excavating it from the land. Since they attempt to decode the history on the land, they might also be called landscape historians.

Although lacking hand callouses and not brandishing excavating trowels (but sometimes suffering foot blisters and usually sporting 35 mm. cameras), above-ground archaeologists share a close kinship with their below-ground counterparts. Like traditional archaeologists, those who study the artifacts still in place concentrate on using material objects and physical sites as primary evidence for doing cultural history. Such landscape historians are naturally committed to extensive fieldwork as a research strategy, and they adapt anthropological research techniques, such as diffusion, where feasible, in order to understand the built environment. Finally, and this is their greatest debt to traditional archaeology, above-ground archaeologists are intent on looking at all objects, be they shards or service stations, with an intense, systematic, and precise scrutiny that ultimately yields specific cultural information from single artifacts as well as broad cultural patterns from larger assemblages of such material culture data.

An above-ground archaeology perspective can be applied to the American road in several ways. However, anyone interested in gaining insight into the historical consequences of our almost constant coming-and-going on, under, and over the American landscape should always try to seek answers to at least three fundamental questions when using the approach. These questions are:

> What have been the different *purposes* for which Americans have built roads?
> How have changing types of *transport* influenced the development of roads?
> What new roadside *structures* have been created either by or for the road?

Early Road Rationale and Typology

When attempting to decide how a certain road may have first begun, the above-ground archaeologist should distinguish between roads that men have deliberately made and roads that may have simply grown from favorable landforms and topographical conditions. Some of the oldest American roads follow geological history rather than precise man-made orientations. For example, the retreating glaciers of the North American Ice Age bequeathed to the Chicago region a series of physiographic formations that became early Indian roads and later major city streets and metropolitan highways. As the great ice sheet receded irregularly, it occasionally paused long enough to permit shore currents to create spits, bars, even islands (surviving in place-names such as Stoney Island and Blue Island in Chicago), and beaches, as well as a spoke-like pattern of drainage beds radiating from the mouth of the Chicago River. In later times, these sandy strips were the only well-drained ground in the spring, and Indian tribes used them for overland travel when the surrounding area was waterlogged. On a present-day road map of Chicago, the landscape historian recognizes these early "natural roads" as those major diagonal streets that deviate from the city's general rectangular plan: Clark Street and Ridge, Milwaukee, Archer, and Vincennes avenues are all fossils of old glacial formations and early Indian trails.

Roads initially formed by nature's geography—the Iroquois Trail (present New York Route 5), the Wilderness Road (U.S. 25 through the Cumberland Gap), Columbus Street (a former shoreline) in San Francisco's North Beach neighborhood, are other examples —frequently survive as the sites for later, deliberately planned roads, designed for military, commercial, or settlement purposes. A Chicago road map again provides us with a striking example of this phenomenon. Looking at the cluster of roads sandwiched into the narrow space along the south branch of the Chicago River (e.g., from Cermak Road to 95th Street), one can quickly see the historical modes of the city's past transportation types in a horizontal stratigraphy across the map. Within a mile's space, on either side of Interstate 55, are a former glacial streambed (ca. 13,500 years old); an Illini Indian foot trail (ca. A.D. 1400-1600); the portage route of the French *coureurs de bois* (ca. 1793); a nineteenth-century drover trail and plank road that became Archer Avenue (ca. 1840) and was immortalized by Finley Peter Dunne as the tavern site of "Mr. Dooley"; the path of the Illinois and Michigan Canal (ca. 1848); and the roadbed of the Chicago and Alton Railroad (ca. 1860). In this dense transportation corridor, all these artifacts surround the most recent road pattern, I-55, which, as a branch of the Federal Interstate and Defense System, owes part of its origin to the Cold War, being a planned military evacuation route in time of nuclear holocaust.

In this one location we have instances of practically every functional type of road that we are likely to find elsewhere on the American land. There are the early *explorer* or *Indian trails*—examples elsewhere would include Zane's Trace in Ohio (U.S. 22), Bozeman's Trail in Montana (I-94), and, of course, Lewis and Clark's trail across much of the upper western United States. We have the *military* or *governmental* road, also still evident in many other parts of the country: for example, various portions of the El Camino Real—the Royal Highway of the seventeenth-century Spanish conquistadors, east (U.S. 90) to St. Augustine, Florida, and northwest (U.S. 101) to Sonoma, California; General Braddock's (U.S. 40) and General Forbes's (U.S. 30) eighteenth-century roads hacked across Pennsylvania; General Jackson's 516-mile Natchez Trace (Natchez Parkway), a military road of the early nineteenth century. The Albany Post Road (U.S. 9) in New York and the Boston Post Road (U.S. 1) in New England are additional examples of former government roads still evident in local place-names.

Military and government roads in America also usually served as *emigration roads* and *freight roads*. In the first instance, consider how different American history might be without the Oregon Trail (U.S. 30), the Santa Fe Trail (I-25), or the Mormon Trail (I-80). Above-ground archaeologists also recognize that emigration roads, in turn, functioned in the exchange of goods as well as of people, and that some early roads, like the Illinois drover's road, were specifically designed to move rather specialized freight. Jesse Chisholm's Trail, running some eight hundred miles from San Antonio to Abilene, paralleled by present-day I-35, is probably the best-known drover trail in American history and folksong, but others, such as the Magdalena Stock Driveway in Socorro County, New Mexico, were also important roads designed especially for livestock traffic.

Place-names in Maryland and Virginia also alert us to another early mode of transporting products along

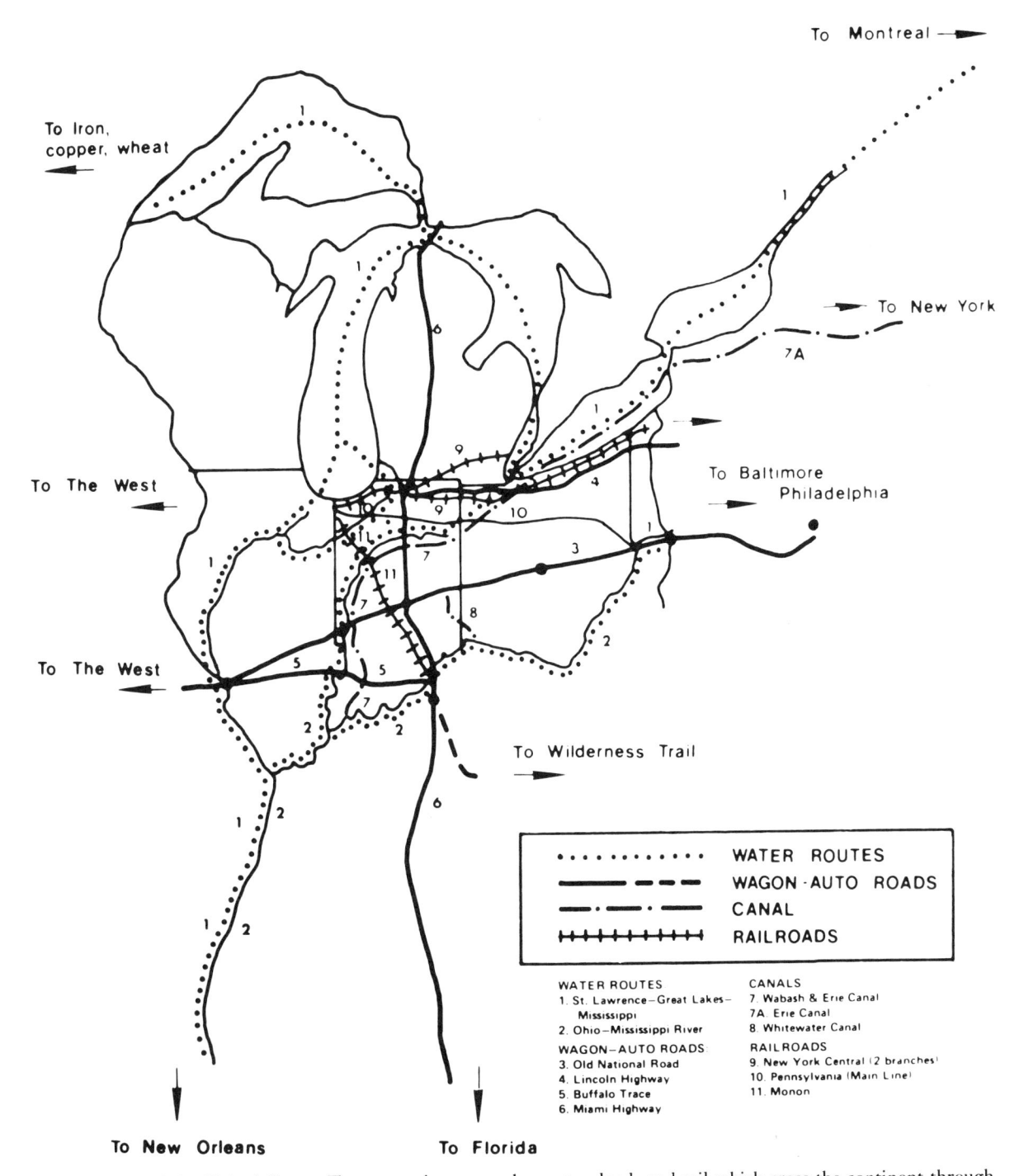

Crossroads of the United States: Transportation routes by water, land, and rail which cross the continent through Indiana. *E. A. Seemann Publishing, Inc.*

special transportation routes. When, in Maryland, one comes upon the name "Rolling Road" (Maryland Route 46), beginning in Rockdale at Liberty Road and running through Catonsville to Relay, one is on an eighteenth-century tobacco road. Along such roads, tobacco in hogsheads was rolled for a hundred miles or more between inland plantations and storehouses that were close to shipping sites on a river or other navigable body of water. Because dirt and water leaking through the staves of the casks could damage the tobacco, it was the practice of the rollers to follow the high ground that separated the region's watersheds and, where possible, to head streams, thus avoiding wetting the tobacco at creek crossings and at fords. Albert Rose, in his tracing of *Historic American Roads: From Frontier Trails to Superhighways* (1976), thought this custom might account, in part, "for many of the meandering country roads in Virginia and other southern states." One of the most widely publicized tobacco-rolling roads in the twentieth century connected northern Georgia with the nearest port on the Savannah River, downstream from the shoals a few miles south of Augusta. Although not as old as those in Virginia, this Georgia tobacco-rolling road has been made famous in American literature by Erskine Caldwell's 1932 novel, *Tobacco Road*, and play (1939) of the same name.

The "New Road" of the Automobile

The presence of the rail*road* (a term Americans prefer rather than rail*way* used in many other countries) on the Chicago map that we have been examining recalls how that transportation mode temporarily eclipsed other road types during much of the nineteenth century. Even as enterprises such as an early *toll road* system and then the federally financed National Road were emerging as road types in the early nineteenth century, their construction was seriously curtailed for much of the next fifty years by a boom in railroad expansion all across the country. By the 1890s, however, several factors prompted a revival of interest in surface travel, resulting in what its advocates often referred to as the "good roads movement." Pressure to improve American thoroughfares came from the League of American Wheelmen who, after the invention of the pneumatic-tire "safety" bicycle in 1885, argued for hard-surfaced roads, even to the point of paying for them. Through magazines such as the *L.A.W. Bulletin* and *Good Roads*, a national Committee on Highway Improvement, and the allocation of funds to pave roads and create bicycle paths in cities, the Wheelmen became the first major national organization to advocate an improved road system as an alternative to the country's railroad network. As will be suggested momentarily, the 1890s also saw numerous innovations in road surfacing and road engineering, as well as, by 1896, the first experimental routes for the Rural Free Delivery of United States mail in West Virginia (the home state of William L. Wilson, the then current postmaster general). Subsequent demand for the extension of RFD gave a tremendous impetus to new road construction, because a prerequisite for service was a gravel or macadam road.

Such interest in expanded road building by private citizens (especially owners and manufacturers of bicycles and autos), lobbying groups such as the American Wheelmen, and various government officials promoted the creation of what geographer J. Todd Snow, writing in *Landscape* (1967), calls "The 'New Road' in the United States." A synonym for this "New Road" would be the *automobile road*, since it is the major change prompted by the largely privately owned, high-speed, personal transport that produced a new road type quite different from other roads that the above-ground archaeologist encounters from the pre-twentieth-century past. In fact, Snow argues that this automobile road is drastically different from most previous roads, particularly in its form and size. As will be suggested later, the U.S. 40 route can be considered

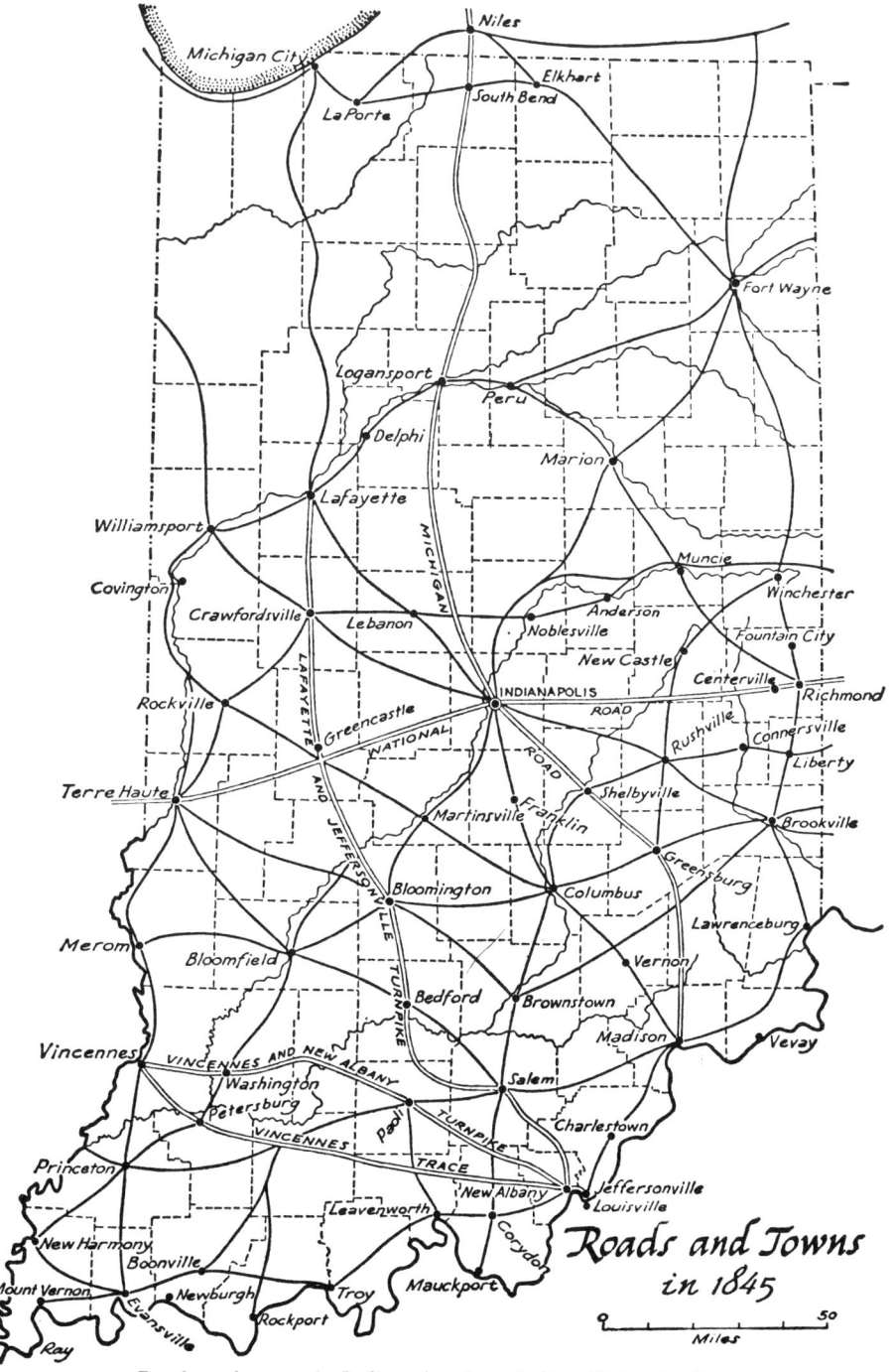

Roads and towns in Indiana in 1845. *Indiana University Press.*

both one of its prototypes and one of its outstanding exemplars.

The early rationale for the "New Road" was primarily recreational. Late nineteenth-century technology had produced two new toys, the bicycle (Fig. 1) and the automobile, both requiring durable, smooth, and continuous surfaces for maximum enjoyment. There were other reasons, to be sure, for the creation of the modern American highway system, but assuredly one reason behind the development of the new roads at the turn of the twentieth century was that Americans delighted in riding bicycles (five million in use in 1900) and driving the new-fangled "benzine buggies," a number of which were manufactured in Indiana. Whereas the old road owed its primary existence to economic, legal, or military needs, the "New Road's" early activities were initially those of exercise, sport, and recreation.

In America, both the bicycle and the automobile were quickly democratized into a tradition of private ownership. Hence users of the "New Road" in this country rapidly came to represent a larger and larger percentage of the national population. Moreover, with the widespread use of the private automobile, overland travel in the United States became also distinctive in at least one important way: traction was by wheel, and speed eventually became very high. These demands greatly altered the surface and configuration of the road, since they required long curves, low gradients, smooth pavement, multiple lanes, and elaborate patterns of controlling access.

The new or automotive road had, of course, many antecedents in older road types, particularly in purpose and function. There were, however, important differences. For example, the impact on the landscape of most automotive roads is different. Where an old road had "followed" or merely "scarred" the land, the "New Road" actually changes it. Valleys are raised, mountains lowered, forests rooted out, streams bridged, properties divided. Road engineering and road surfacing also play a much larger role in the automotive road. Also, the very pervasiveness of the automobile road tends to make it a more dominant feature of the landscape.

The above-ground archaeologist must be cognizant of these new features of the American road. He or she should also attempt to ascertain the cultural behavior behind such material culture. One might test, for instance, hypotheses such as: Does the "New Road," though financed by state and federal funds, foster the same social contact and intercourse as did older modes of local and country roads? Is the "roadside" (with its natural and man-made features) of the "New Road" appreciably different from that which we find along older travel routes? What has the control of access (by means of laws, fences, speed, directionality, multiple lanes) on the "New Road" meant in terms of control of behavior?

To probe such questions, we need a typology of the modern American road system as well as a knowledge of the basic documentary resources for doing highway history. In the latter case, several works are invaluable to understanding the twentieth-century roadscape: Albert C. Rose's *Historic American Roads* (1976), the U.S. Department of Transportation's *American Highways, 1776-1976* (1976), and *Highways in Our National Life*, edited by Jean Labatut and Wheaton J. Lane (1950) are important overviews that the above-ground archaeologist should consult as useful reference tools.

How might we develop a tentative typology for the new or automobile road? Where might we find appropriate examples of the evolution of its principal features? How might such road types be viewed as cultural indicators of American values?

Perhaps the first "New Road" type of which the above-ground archaeologist should be aware is that one promoted by the private road organizations throughout the first two decades of the twentieth century: the trail association highway. In the absence of any governmental action, private commercial pro-

Fig. 1. Participants in a Franklin Bicycle Race posing in front of Ben Winans' printery in Brookville, Indiana, 1896. *IHS*.

moters linked together strings of existing roads on maps, occasionally raised funds to surface parts of them, and gave them distinctive names. The routes were often physically marked by bands of different colors on telephone poles and other signposts. A 1922 Rand McNally road map of Indiana suggests the wide extent of such routes in their heyday in the early 1920s. All over the country merchants and restaurant and hotel owners paid promoters to route these highways past their places of business. The promoters of roads such as the Old Spanish Trail, the Cody-Billings Way, the Victory Highway, the Bankhead Highway, the Red Arrow Highway, in turn, made their roads into advertising devices by identifying their routes with distinctive colors and symbols painted on buildings or trees, or affixed to fences and signposts along the way.

The observant traveler can still find artifactual

evidence of these private highways in the typonymy of extant businesses along their routes as well as in local street, road, and place-names. In South Bend, Indiana, for example, one finds U.S. 31 named "Dixieway" or the "Dixie Highway," reminding us of Carl G. Fisher's Dixie Highway Association that, in 1914, mapped a 5,706-mile road which ran from Ontario (Canada) to Miami (Florida). Fisher (Fig. 2), a president of the Indianapolis Motor Speedway, having purchased a winter home in Florida during the land boom of the early twentieth century, wanted to be able to drive "a way down south to Dixie" without being sidetracked.

The Lincoln Highway Association, another brainstorm of Fisher's, was probably the most famous of the highway association roads of the 1910s. Supported by automobile manfacturers in the Midwest, this "Coast-to-Coast Highway" was conceived in 1913 with the aim of building a great transcontinental object-lesson road at a time when there were few improved long-distance highways in the United States. With the goal of linking New York with San Francisco via the best and most direct route across the midsection of the country, the Lincoln Highway, for the greater portion of its original 3,389-mile length, coincided with present U.S. Route 30. While the primary purpose of the association was to connect existing roads into a transcontinental corridor and to promote (but usually not actually build) new highways where gaps occurred along the route, a fragment of its program for an "Ideal Section" of the Lincoln Highway, built in 1922, can still be seen in Lake County (Indiana), running west of Dyer on the Illinois-Indiana state boundary.

As disconnected sections of improved roads were joined into continuous long-distance routes, many travelers became bewildered by the motley array of, and often highly confusing, directional and informational signs encountered in the different states. In the neighborhood of their home towns motorists could find their way in spite of the crude or missing direction signs. On a long journey in unfamiliar localities,

Fig. 2. Carl G. Fisher, founder of the Indianapolis Motor Speedway and developer and promoter of the Lincoln Highway and Dixie Highway. *Indianapolis Star-News.*

however, a lack of consistent information became a source of continual delay, uncertainty, and confusion. It was to bring order out of this chaos of signs, and thus help to speed the tourist upon his way, that the American Association of State Highway Officials, an organization founded in 1914 to promote cooperation between state and federal governments regarding highways, suggested a plan for marking the main roads of the country with standardized information and direction signs. At the request of the association, the secretary of agriculture, on March 2, 1925, appointed a Joint Board of State and Federal Highway Officials, "to undertake immediately the selection and designation of a comprehensive system of through interstate routes, and to devise a comprehensive and uniform scheme for designating such routes in such manner as to give them a conspicuous place among the highways of the country as roads of interstate and national significance."

This Joint Board requested the respective state highway departments to select the routes within their own borders to be included in such a system and then reviewed these recommendations at regional and national conferences. Subsequently a nationwide coordinated system throughout the forty-eight states was designated. This network became the newest manifestation of the "New Road": the numbered federal highway system of the 1920s.

The numbers assigned to the routes by the Joint Board had a special significance. Even numbers were assigned to the east-west roads and odd numbers to the highways running in a north-south direction. The more important transcontinental routes were designated in multiples of ten beginning at U.S. Route 10, in the northern United States, and ending with Route 90, traversing the southern states from coast to coast.

Fig. 3. Direction signs on U.S. 50 west of Shoals, Indiana, 1930. *Indiana State Highway Commission.*

Fig. 4. Maze of road signs in downtown Terre Haute, Indiana, looking west on Wabash Avenue (U.S. 40) at its intersection with U.S. 41 and 150 and State Road 63, 1981. *IHS—Seldon Bradley.*

North-and-south roads began with U.S. 1 along the Atlantic seaboard and the numbers increased towards the west until the road along the Pacific Coast was enumerated as U.S. Route 101. A uniform number marker was adopted, still in use today, consisting of a shield, on the face of which are the initials U.S., the number of the route, and (on older signs) the name of the state in black on a white base. The Joint Board also agreed upon a standard design for rectangular direction signs, with black letters superimposed upon a white background. The standard United States shield number markers are easily distinguishable from the state route markers emblazoned, for example, with a covered wagon for Nebraska or the state's geographical outline for Indiana.

Several documentary studies aid in our contemporary above-ground archaeological investigation of the major U.S. highways numbered in the 1920s. In addition to the Federal Writers' Project American Guide Series on Routes 1, 101, and 66, we also have George Stewart's classic trek across U.S. 40, *U.S. 40—Cross Section of the United States of America*, and now a delightful survey of North Carolina's Highway 64 by Linda Dahl, Tracy Segner, and Whitney Talcott in *Carolina Dwelling* (1978), a valuable guide to that state's vernacular roadside environment. These U.S. routes, however, have no formal status by law. According to an official bulletin of the Public Roads Administration, "the designation as a U.S. route is without legal or administrative significance." Such routes are designated and numbered merely "for the convenience of mapmakers, information services, and highway travelers." Hence, a system designed to eliminate chaos still tends to perpetuate a slight degree of confusion, in that the above-ground archaeologist will find that no one seems to be sure whether, for example, the correct usage is "U.S. Highway 40" or "U.S. Route 40," or the simple colloquial "U.S. 40."

Similar semantic confusion results when the landscape analyst attempts to unravel the history of parkways, freeways, and expressways—other manifestations of the twentieth-century highway. The terms are, unfortunately, often used interchangeably, when, in fact, each can be distinguished as separate historical features of the evolving American roadscape. The designation *parkway* appears to be the oldest term, and usually has been distinguished by a central dividing strip of landscaped ground, which originated as a formal element in civic or spatial compositions such as the double roadway laid out (1699) in the Green before the Governor's Palace at Williamsburg, Virginia; the Elm Street designed (1838) in Manchester, New Hampshire; or Commonwealth Avenue in Boston (1858). In the nineteenth century, the landscape architect Frederick Law Olmsted popularized the parkway concept in many of his landscape plans. In his pioneer Central Park (1857) and especially in his plans for the environs surrounding Brooklyn's Prospect Park (1868), Olmsted recommended that cities build a series of parkways, roads with large strips of parkland on either side that would maintain the parklike amenities of their outlying suburban region. In a 1980 article in the *Journal of Urban History* tracing the development of "The Urban Parkway, 1900-1940," urban historian Clay McShane notes that Olmsted's design, the model for those he and others would construct elsewhere (e.g., the Eastern Parkway in Brooklyn; the Harlem River Drive in New York City; the Rock Creek Parkway in Washington, D.C.; the South Park District in Chicago, particularly its Midway Plaisance), served three major functions: recreation, high speed travel, and transportation routes for upper class neighborhoods.

Since the parkway was originally forbidden to public vehicles, such as omnibuses, wagons, and street railways, it would also be a pleasure drive for private carriage owners. Olmsted believed that such a parkway would maximize the benefits of public parks by bringing recreational land along its margin within reach of a larger population than would have access to a centrally located park. He believed that such a road would also facilitate downtown travel by private carriage, since it would have no slow-moving traffic and few cross streets cutting through its progress. The park strips on either side of the road would additionally cut off much local traffic. English common law by tradition had held that governments must provide access to all roads for abutters, but since the new-style parkway had strips of park, not residences or businesses directly alongside it, access could be limited. Such limitation of access was the key to the parkway concept.

Robert Moses, perhaps one of the most influential molders of the modern American landscape, not only in the metropolitan New York region where he was city planner for almost half a century, but also elsewhere where his concepts of massive urban planning have been imitated, used the parkway idea in various ways. For instance, he pioneered the concept of opening new parks at the ends of his parkways, most notably Jones Beach, one of the best-known public beaches in the United States. The landscape historian can also perceive Moses's social and political philosophy, as well as the effects of spatial design's impact on the economic, racial, and social history of a city, in the road systems he put in place on Long Island. Robert A. Caro, in his biography, *The Power Broker: Robert Moses and the Fall of New York* (1975), shows how Moses, realizing that his parkways enhanced land values, used them to create middle- and upper-class enclaves. His Long Island roads excluded public transportation, effectively reserving the new suburbs for auto owners. Moses feared that some future generation of politicians might reverse this ban and eliminate the zoning restrictions along the new highways. To counter this, he developed an innovative engineering solution. Ostensibly for aesthetic purposes, the Long Island State Park Commission engineers used only arch bridges for overpasses on its parkways. The arches had a height of only eleven feet at the curb, two feet lower than the height of buses, thus guaranteeing Moses's wish that the roads remain for auto use only. Automobile owners of the "upper" and "comfortable middle" classes (as Moses called them) had almost unlimited access to the parkways for recreation and commuting. Poor people, who normally used public transit, were kept off such roads because the twelve-foot-tall buses could not get through the overpasses.

Under the aegis of New Deal programs such as the Works Progress Administration (WPA) and Public Works Administration (PWA), American city and highway planners developed the parkway concept in two directions—one rural, the other urban. The artifactual legacy of the first trend includes the ten national parkways developed by the National Park Service. Beginning in 1933 with the Skyline Drive, located high in the Blue Ridge Mountains of Virginia, and continuing with current projects such as the Foothills Parkway in Tennessee, these scenic parkways, interestingly enough, occasionally retrace historic explorer trails and travel routes, such as the Natchez Trail Parkway connecting Nashville (Tennessee) and Natchez (Mississippi).

City planners, like Robert Moses, while still using the term "parkway" began in the 1930s to move toward the development of what has been called the *urban expressway* or *freeway*, a landscape feature now common to many American metropolitan areas. A freeway is usually defined as a road of any physical standard that has access limited by the state or country. Thus, technically, a gravel road without separated intersections can be a freeway. Frequently included in the definition of the road is that it is "free from tolls." However, we usually now associate the term with major urban highways such as the freeway network developed in a state such as California. In his study of *Freeways* (1966), Lawrence Halprin provides us with a basic classification system for identifying such artifacts (Fig. 5). For example, there are at-grade freeways, depressed freeways, tunneled freeways, as well as several variants (e.g., stacked, embanked, side-by-side) of the elevated freeway.

Much of the impetus for this contemporary history on the land again came from the federal treasury. Moses, for example, used his hefty slice of WPA funds to extend the Long Island and Westchester Parkway systems into the heart of downtown New York. Other cities quickly followed suit. These roads differed considerably from the earlier parkways from which they were derived, in that, while commercial traffic was often not allowed, the park strips on their sides dwindled away to as little as five feet in places. Eventually even these landscape amenities were eliminated, and the modern multilane, limited access, totally concrete ribbon known as the urban freeway became a pervasive landscape component of American cities. In addition to arguing that the freeway would solve the dilemmas of continually expanding vehicular traffic (especially truck freight), city planners took advantage of United States involvement in World War II by advocating the construction of such urban limited-access roads for civil defense purposes, claiming that they would facilitate evacuation in case of air raids (precisely the justification that the federal government would later use in justifying urban extensions of the Interstate system).

In order to understand the historical background of the expressway, the above-ground archaeologist should be familiar with its basic, successive innovations in design, layout, and construction. One general clue to the character of the contemporary expressway is the fact that many of its features originated with the railroad rather than the highway. Railroads had developed before the end of the nineteenth century various

Fig. 5. The Madison Avenue expressway in Indianapolis, ca. 1958, an example of separation of different types of traffic. *Ray Bright, IHS.*

Fig. 6. Traffic delay at railroad crossing on Kentucky Avenue in Indianapolis, ca. 1948. *National Archives and Records Service.*

special devices for the efficient and expeditious movement of high-speed traffic. By the second quarter of the twentieth century, these innovations began to appear in a systematic way on American highways.

In addition to the adoption of certain railroad signaling systems (which had been used for governing train movements through junction crossings) to control the flow of vehicular traffic (e.g., overhead lane control signals first used in 1927 for the New Jersey approach to the Holland Tunnel in New York), highway engineers borrowed many ideas from railroad track layout plans in order to separate different types of traffic. As Carl Condit points out in his valuable reference work to *American Building Art: The Twentieth Century* (1961), where the complexity of intersecting lines required it, the railroad had developed multilevel grade separations that embraced features later to be employed in highway planning, such as the famous "Spaghetti Bowl" Chicago Circle intersection of eight highways on the city's west side. In addition, there are many places where rail freight traffic is separated from passenger traffic, and through traffic from local—all by the device of parallel lines, a practice replicated in a number of Los Angeles freeways. Double-deck rail routes are characteristic of certain bridges and their approaches, a trait the landscape observer also finds in

16   U.S. 40: A ROADSCAPE OF THE AMERICAN EXPERIENCE

Chicago's Wacker Drive (1921-25) and Jersey City's Holland Tunnel. Continuous elevated track represents the most straightforward solution to the urban problem of removing the railroad right-of-way from all forms of different or conflicting traffic, and it has its highway parallel in roads such as the Pulaski Skyway (1929-32) in the Newark-Jersey City area of northern New Jersey, the West Side Expressway (1928-38) on Manhattan Island, and the Chicago Skyway.

Railroads developed a number of techniques in their quest for interchange systems, including unidirectional crossings and fly-over junctions. Highway planners, recognizing their similar problem of separating, without stopping, conflicting streams of high-speed traffic at intersections, followed the railroads' lead, but were forced to use greater amounts of land in implementing their ideas. They first employed the traffic circle (Fig. 8), a concept invented by Holroyd Smith of London, England, in 1907 and popular for a time in New Jersey, parts of New England, and, by necessity because of multiple intersections, in Washington, D.C., and in Indianapolis around Monument Circle. Dissatisfaction with the hazards and delays of the circle when applied to high-speed freeway roads led to the development of the double-level cloverleaf interchange, an idea first proposed in 1906 by Eugene Henard, a Parisian engineer, and patented in 1916 in the United States by Arthur Hale of Baltimore. The cloverleaf saw its first practical application in 1928 at the intersection of State Highways 4 and 25 in Woodbridge, New Jersey, and was later employed systematically in a succession of intersections along the upper half of Chicago's North Lake Shore Drive (1930-33). (See Figs. 9 and 10.)

A number of twentieth-century highways, while being distinctly "New Road" types, recalled older transportation configurations when they were also defined as *toll roads* and *turnpikes*. The first turnpike built in this country was the Little River Turnpike constructed in Virginia in 1785. With the advent of the railroad and the development of "shunpikes" (roads devised so that the user could avoid paying tolls on the turnpike), these toll roads fell into disuse and are often remembered only by relict place-names such as Toll

Fig. 7. Railroad grade separation at the same crossing on Kentucky Avenue (Fig. 6), ca. 1950. *National Archives and Records Service.*

Fig. 8. Traffic circle in Elizabeth, New Jersey, ca. 1940. *National Archives and Records Service.*

Gate (West Virginia), Toll House (California), and any number of local roads and city streets still designated as "pikes." In the 1930s, however, the concept of the toll road was revived by municipalities, states, and the federal government. We still have the artifacts of this second turnpike boom very much with us. It is ironic, for example, that the state of Pennsylvania would use the right-of-way of the abandoned South Penn Railroad on which to build a new toll road, the first section of the Pennsylvania Turnpike, between Harrisburg and Pittsburgh in 1940. Over the next three decades, fifty new toll roads in more than twenty states added mileage to this "New Road" type. The Northern Indiana Toll Road (Figs. 11 and 12), opened all across the state by 1957, was Indiana's contribution to the post-World War II turnpike boom.

The Pennsylvania Turnpike is likewise a prototype for the last major road type that the above-ground archaeologist must understand: that is, the modern high-speed *interstate highway.* Now also known as U.S. Interstate 70/76 over much of its length, the Pennsylvania Turnpike incorporated the most advanced designs of German and American engineers on highway grades and curvature. Its rapid construction—a 160-mile toll road built in less than two years through the Appalachian Mountains—prompted renewed interest in a longstanding American aspiration—the establishment of a comprehensive interstate road system. Proposed as early as the building of the National Road through the Northwest Territory, further stim-

18 U.S. 40: A ROADSCAPE OF THE AMERICAN EXPERIENCE

Fig. 9. Cloverleafs on Lake Shore Drive, Chicago, ca. 1940. *National Archives and Records Service.*

ulated by military planning of roads for national defense (such as in the Pershing Map of 1922, the 1,480 mile Alaskan Highway of 1943, and the rural interstate evacuation highway system of 1945), the drive for a truly national program of interstate roads culminated in the Federal Interstate Highway Act of 1956, which created the National System of Interstate and Defense Highways. The project was first budgeted at $25 billion, 90 percent of it to be paid by the federal government and 10 percent by the states, with construction initially authorized through fiscal year 1969. To date, the 42,500-mile interstate system is still building, having cost American taxpayers $90 billion and having altered the rural and urban landscape in many unprecedented ways. Receiving the largest transportation subsidy from the national government since the building of the nineteenth-century railroads, the interstate system, with its thousands of bridges, interchanges, traffic separators, cloverleafs, rest areas, overpasses, and tunnels, is assuredly one of contemporary America's most extensive artifact assemblages.

The elaborate interstate system, like the many other types of the twentieth-century American highways, deserves careful study as an important index to our recent history. In government documents such as the Bureau of Public Road's *Toll Roads and Free Roads* (1939) and *A Ten-Year National Highway Program* (1955), and in recent appraisals like David Brodsley's *L.A. Freeway* (1981) and Mark H. Rose's *Interstate: Express Highway Politics* (1979), we find part of the data

Fig. 10. Interchange construction at the intersection of Shadeland Avenue and U.S. 40, on the east side of Indianapolis, 1958. *Ray Bright, IHS.*

Fig. 11. Ground breaking ceremony for the Indiana Toll Road near South Bend, Indiana, September 21, 1954. *Indiana Toll Road Commission.*

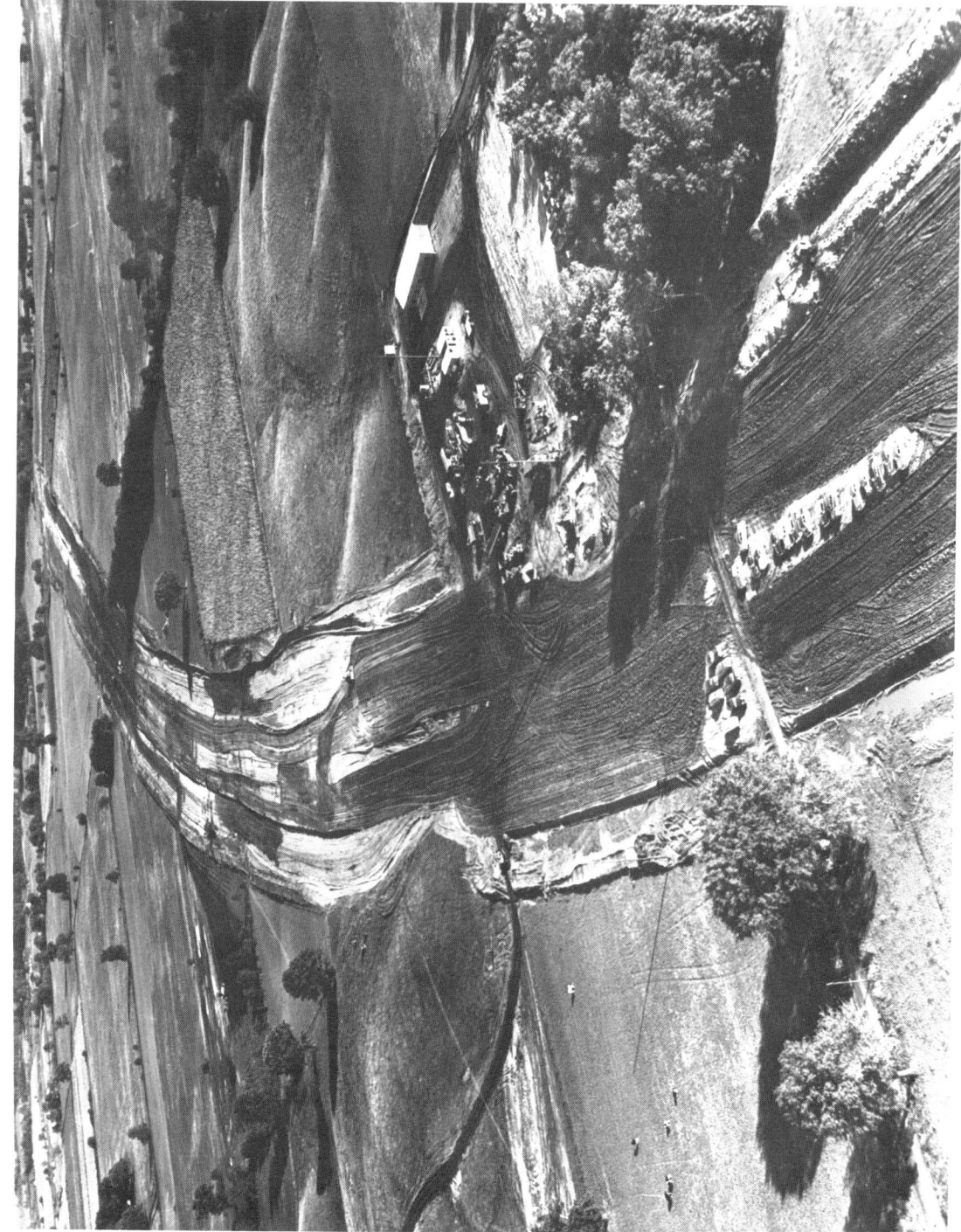

Fig. 12. Construction of the Indiana Toll Road in St. Joseph County, Indiana. *Indiana Toll Road Commission.*

to understand this history. However, much more of this story of changing ideas about land use, civil engineering, mobility, recreation, and economic growth is to be found outside our automobile window and in our rear-view mirrors.

Road Engineering and Road Controls

Most roads must cross watercourses and other natural obstacles that they encounter en route if they are to continue to their destinations. Creeks, rivers, estuaries, and the arms of the sea, as well as tidal marshes, swamps, gorges, ravines, and escarpments—any one of these could bring a road to its end. In the early stages of road building, whenever the route encountered a watercourse such as a river or stream, the road developer had several options. First, he might abandon the overland route and proceed by water, a decision that accounts for the historical development of cities such as Portage, Wisconsin, or Grand Portage, Minnesota. A second alternative would be to continue the surface road along the banks of the watercourse, the historical origin of many of our river or shore roads, such as the famous Platte River Road in Nebraska or the Wabash River Road in Indiana. A third option would be to cross the watercourse either by fording it (hence the origin of settlements like Chadds Ford in Pennsylvania or Leiters Ford in Indiana), or by establishing a ferry service (the beginnings of Harpers Ferry in West Virginia), or by constructing a bridge across it.

When roads began to carry an increased volume of heavy traffic that included horse-drawn vehicles and therefore made footbridges impractical, the bridging of America was underway, first with wood and stone, later with iron, steel, and concrete. Its legacy is the several thousand bridges, large and small, that give continuity to the American road and provide the above-ground archaeologist with a category of artifactual evidence worthy of careful study and interpretation.

Bridges figure prominently in American history, and not just as examples of American road engineering. Pitched battles, such as the one at Concord, Massachusetts, have been fought on them. Settlement patterns have been shaped by them: consider spans such as the 1939 Bayonne Bridge crossing the Kill van Kull, connecting Staten Island with New Jersey, which drastically changed neighborhoods in both communities. Similarly changes happened with the opening of the Golden Gate Bridge in San Francisco. Artifacts have been spawned by them: bridges like the 1883 Brooklyn Bridge crossing New York's East River inspired the paintings of Joseph Stella and John Marin, the photography of Bernice Abbott and David Plowden, the autobiographical writing of Alfred Kazin, and the epic poetry ("The Bridge") of Hart Crane. But before the bridge could inspire, influence, or incite, it had to *be*, and that being has also its own detailed history.

Above-ground archaeologists with special interests in American bridges have organized into at least one general organization (the American Society for Industrial Archaeology), and one more specialized society (the National Society for the Preservation of Covered Bridges). Many Americans would probably accord most of the thousand covered bridges in the United States a degree of historical status.

How does the historian of the landscape keep track of American bridge types? Among fixed or stationary bridges, how do we distinguish a simple beam from a simple truss? a cantilever from a suspension span? What is the historical difference between bascule, swing, pontoon, and vertical lift bridges in addition to their all being movable artifacts? Fortunately, T. Allan Comp, the senior historian for the Historic American Engineering Record (HAER), and Donald Jackson, a civil engineer on the HAER staff, have prepared a superb field guide, *Bridge Truss Types: A Guide to Dating and Identifying* (1977), to assist the beginning fieldworker. The authors provide simple

Fig. 13. Bridge on the old National Road (later U.S. 40) over White River in Indianapolis in the 1840s and 1850s. Drawing by Christian Schrader. *Indiana State Library*.

Fig. 14. Bridge on U.S. 40 over White River in Indianapolis, ca. 1920. *Bass Photo*.

24   U.S. 40: A ROADSCAPE OF THE AMERICAN EXPERIENCE

diagrams (see Figs. 15 and 16) and cogent, comprehensive technical explanations, along with photographs of many extant bridges for field identification and comparison.

In order to construct a similar primer for other bridge types, the above-ground archaeologist should turn to Carl Condit's two-volume *American Building Art* (1960-61), Henry Fraham Tyrrell's *History of Bridge Engineering* (1911), or H. J. Hopkins, *A Span of Bridges* (1970). David Plowden's photographic tribute to *Bridges, The Spans of North America* (1974) is also helpful for making visual identification in the field.

Above-ground archaeologist David L. Weitzman shows how a seemingly nondescript bridge in northern California can be analyzed. Writing in *Historic Preservation* (November-December 1979) about "A Conversation with Bridge 3," Weitzman demonstrates how an out-of-the-way, 150-foot span that local people call the Burger Creek Bridge and that Mendocino County engineers and road crews know simply as "bridge 3, road 322," is an actual history text in rivets and girders.

"Much of bridge 3's history is right there," claims Weitzman.

> You need only a couple of simple rules of thumb, an understanding of the meaning of a detail or two and, most important, some historical imagination to read it. The name of the fabricator—Phoenix Bridge Company, Phoenixville, Pennsylvania—can be read plainly in the cast- and wrought-iron members. If there were no foundry mark, you would look for a small oval or rectangular builder's plate, usually on one of the end posts or crowning the bridge high atop the portal struts at each end. This might include a date, but there is none on bridge 3. The bridge dates itself in the way its components—top and bottom chords, vertical posts, diagonals and end posts—are fastened together with large nuts and bolts, 'pins,' as they are known to engineers. Before about 1890, virtually every bridge was assembled in this way. By 1920, however, this practice had all but disappeared, the now familiar rivets and gusset plates replacing the single pin.

Admittedly three decades do not cut a neat line between two periods of bridge design, but other significant, if more subtle, changes were taking place. Bridges were changing not just in detail, but in their overall aspect as well. Girders were used more and more often in place of thin rods and columns. Truss bridges grew heavier, more earthbound, muscular, and much too serious, quite a contrast to the playfulness and style of bridge 3. "Our bridge," concludes Weitzman, "is clearly, albeit subjectively, old, certainly not of this century and probably from before the 1890s."

Weitzman, who has also written a delightful landscape history primer for children titled *Underfoot: An Everyday Guide to Exploring the American Past* (1976), proposes that Bridge 3 has at least one more story to tell the above-ground archaeologist. In his "Conversation with Bridge 3," he writes that the Phoenix firm in Philadelphia

> did not build this bridge for the Dos Rios-Laytonville road . . . . the trusses are impressively deep for their length, 26 feet from the bottom chord to the wooden deck above. Even if this road existed in the 1880s, the few horse-drawn farm wagons and occasional mule train of the day would not call for so large a truss. That delicate tracery of rods is, in fact, the mark of a Whipple-Murphy truss (sometimes called a double-intersection Pratt), one of the most popular bridge designs of the last century—for *railroads*. Only one kind of vehicle demanded trusses like those now spanning Burger Creek: railroad locomotives which, by the 1890s, were approaching 100 tons! A talk with local historians and a search through the files of the county public works department revealed that bridge 3 is in a new life after retirement. Like so many other bridges still around, this one started out on the railroad, the Northwestern Pacific mainline, and was retired from railroad use in the 1930s when, not incidentally, mainline locomotives weighed in at 200 tons and were still growing.

READING THE ROAD 25

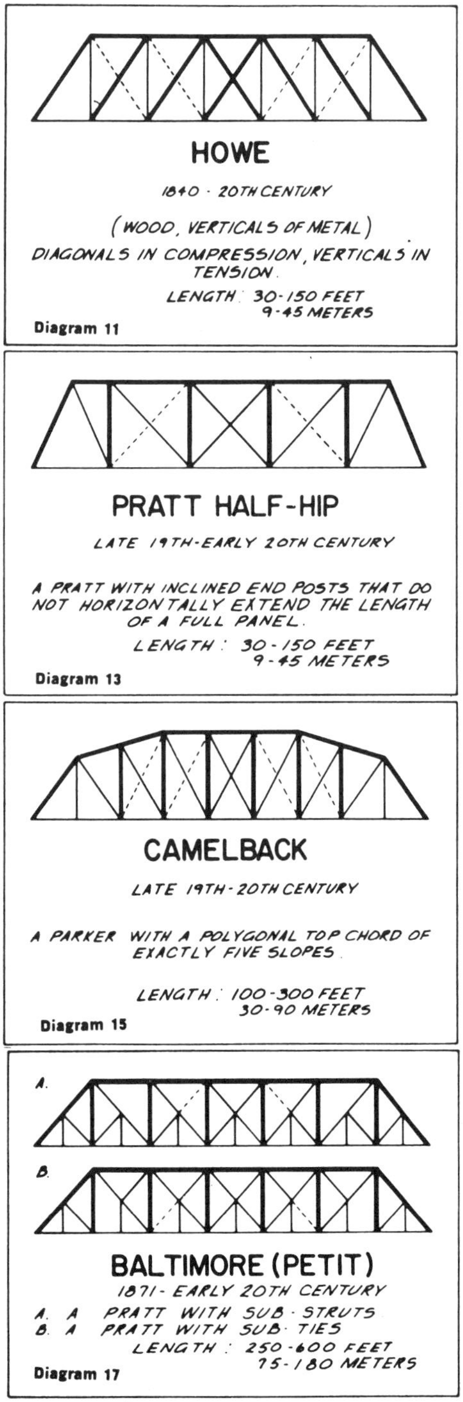

HOWE

1840 - 20TH CENTURY

(WOOD, VERTICALS OF METAL)

DIAGONALS IN COMPRESSION, VERTICALS IN TENSION.

LENGTH: 30-150 FEET
9-45 METERS

Diagram 11

PRATT

1844 - 20TH CENTURY

DIAGONALS IN TENSION, VERTICALS IN COMPRESSION, (EXCEPT FOR HIP VERTICALS ADJACENT TO INCLINED END POSTS).

LENGTH: 25-150 FEET
8-45 METERS

Diagram 12

PRATT HALF-HIP

LATE 19TH-EARLY 20TH CENTURY

A PRATT WITH INCLINED END POSTS THAT DO NOT HORIZONTALLY EXTEND THE LENGTH OF A FULL PANEL.

LENGTH: 30-150 FEET
9-45 METERS

Diagram 13

PARKER

MID-LATE 19TH - 20 CENTURY

A PRATT WITH A POLYGONAL TOP CHORD

LENGTH: 40-200 FEET
12-60 METERS

Diagram 14

CAMELBACK

LATE 19TH - 20TH CENTURY

A PARKER WITH A POLYGONAL TOP CHORD OF EXACTLY FIVE SLOPES.

LENGTH: 100-300 FEET
30-90 METERS

Diagram 15

LENTICULAR (PARABOLIC)

1878 - EARLY 20TH CENTURY

A PRATT WITH BOTH TOP AND BOTTOM CHORDS PARABOLICLY CURVED OVER THEIR ENTIRE LENGTH.

LENGTH: 150-400 FEET
45-120 METERS

Diagram 16

BALTIMORE (PETIT)

1871 - EARLY 20TH CENTURY

A. A PRATT WITH SUB-STRUTS
B. A PRATT WITH SUB-TIES

LENGTH: 250-600 FEET
75-180 METERS

Diagram 17

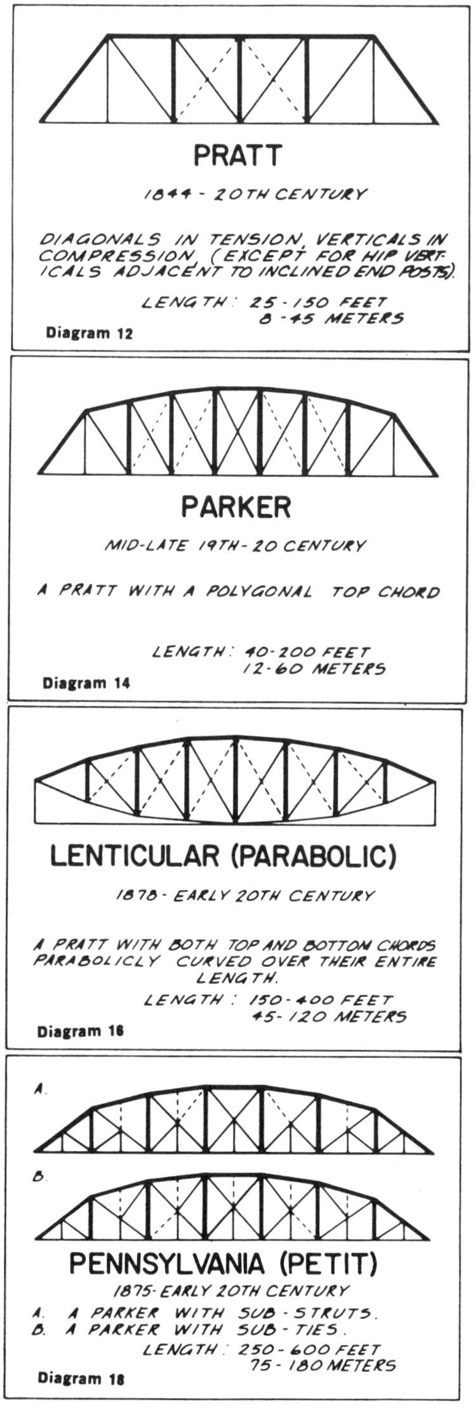

PENNSYLVANIA (PETIT)

1875 - EARLY 20TH CENTURY

A. A PARKER WITH SUB-STRUTS
B. A PARKER WITH SUB-TIES

LENGTH: 250-600 FEET
75-180 METERS

Diagram 18

Figs. 15 (left) and 16 (right). Bridge types.

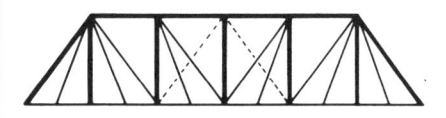

KELLOGG
LATE 19TH CENTURY

A VARIATION ON THE PRATT WITH ADDITIONAL DIAGONALS RUNNING FROM UPPER CHORD PANEL POINTS TO THE CENTER OF THE LOWER CHORDS.

LENGTH: 75-150 FEET
23-30 METERS

Diagram 19

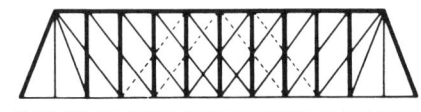

DOUBLE INTERSECTION PRATT
1847- 20TH CENTURY

(WHIPPLE, WHIPPLE-MURPHY, LINVILLE)
AN INCLINED END POST PRATT WITH DIAGONALS THAT EXTEND ACROSS TWO PANELS.

LENGTH: 70- 300 FEET
21-90 METERS

Diagram 20

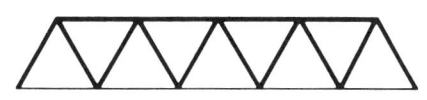

WARREN
1848- 20TH CENTURY

TRIANGULAR IN OUTLINE, THE DIAGONALS CARRY BOTH COMPRESSIVE AND TENSILE FORCES. A TRUE WARREN TRUSS HAS EQUILATERAL TRIANGLES.

LENGTH: 50-400 FEET
15-120 METERS

Diagram 21

WARREN
WITH VERTICALS
MID 19TH- 20TH CENTURY

DIAGONALS CARRY BOTH COMPRESSIVE AND TENSILE FORCES. VERTICALS SERVE AS BRACING FOR TRIANGULAR WEB SYSTEM.

LENGTH: 50-400 FEET
15-120 METERS

Diagram 22

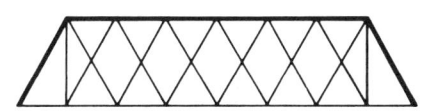

DOUBLE INTERSECTION WARREN
(LATTICE)
MID 19TH- 20TH CENTURY

STRUCTURE IS INDETERMINANT. MEMBERS ACT IN BOTH COMPRESSION AND TENSION. TWO TRIANGULAR WEB SYSTEMS ARE SUPERIMPOSED UPON EACH OTHER WITH OR WITHOUT VERTICALS.

LENGTH: 75-400 FEET
23-120 METERS

Diagram 23

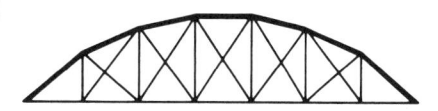

BOWSTRING ARCH-TRUSS
1840- LATE 19TH CENTURY

A TIED ARCH WITH THE DIAGONALS SERVING AS BRACING AND THE VERTICALS SUPPORTING THE DECK.

LENGTH: 70-175 FEET
21-50 METERS

Diagram 24

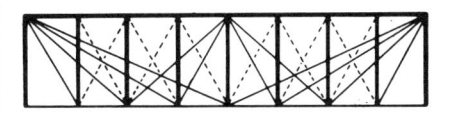

FINK
1851- MID- LATE 19TH CENTURY
(RARE)

VERTICALS IN COMPRESSION, DIAGONALS IN TENSION, LONGEST DIAGONALS RUN FROM END POSTS TO CENTER PANEL POINTS.

LENGTH: 75-100 FEET
23-45 METERS

Diagram 25

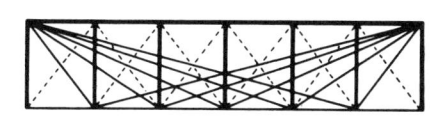

BOLLMAN
1852- MID-LATE 19TH CENTURY
(RARE)

VERTICALS IN COMPRESSION, DIAGONALS IN TENSION. DIAGONALS RUN FROM END POSTS TO EVERY PANEL POINT.

LENGTH: 75-100 FEET
23-30 METERS

Diagram 26

American Association for State and Local History.

With the skill born of practice and patience, anyone can learn to identify and address (if you like) a Whipple-Murphy truss (named for civil engineers Whipple and Murphy), or any other number of bridge types by whose trusses—the (Theodore) Burr, the (James) Warren, the (Wendel) Bollman, the (William) Howe, the (Albert) Fink, the (Ithiel) Town—you shall know them. It may be surprising to learn that bridges, like so much of our landscape material culture, have such personal names, acquired from the early American builder-engineers who patented their designs.

Road surfaces also have personal names and intriguing individual histories (see Fig. 17). For example, John Loudon MacAdam (1756-1836), a Scottish builder and engineer, developed a pavement called "macadam" that was the best type of road surface available for most of the nineteenth century. Consisting of a road base in which clean, broken, or crushed stone was mechanically locked in place by rolling, the roadbed was bonded by small stone particles that were worked into the voids and then "set" with water. First tested in America on the Boonesboro Pike between Hagerstown and Boonesboro, Maryland, in 1832, "the MacAdam principle" was soon applied to seventy-three miles of the National Road, west from the bank of the Ohio River to Zanesville in 1825 and then used frequently along the federal route. Prior to macadam roads, Americans had been using all types of materials—oyster shells, limerock marl, iron ore, caliche, cobbles, slag, corn husks, cinders, chert, and, of course, sand, gravel, and just plain dirt—to create their roadbeds. These locally available surfacing materials, although now covered by concrete, are sometimes betrayed in place-names, such as "Slag Road," "Cinder Trail," or "Gravel Road." And in rural areas of the country, where there still is a minimum amount of high-speed auto traffic, such road surfaces are also still to be found.

Roads paved for any length with planks, bricks, cobblestones, or granite blocks were usually an urban luxury until the 1880s. Most roads were dirt or, in bad weather, mud. The majority of those that were surfaced at all, reported George Waring in the 1880 census, were of gravel or macadam construction. Over the next three decades, however, both the surface and the shape of the American road changed drastically. In 1892, the first brick surface on a rural road in this country was laid on the Wooster Pike near Cleveland in Ohio's Cuyahoga County. Dust palliatives (Fig. 18) began to be applied to road surfaces as early as the 1890s when Los Angeles County officials first used crude petroleum oil to quell the dust clouds raised by passing autos. By 1905 coal tar and other bituminous substances were being experimented with by the Madison Good Roads Commission in Jackson, Tennessee, as well as the Rhode Island Board of Public Roads. Early uses of Portland cement took place in 1893 in Bellefontaine, Ohio (where one can still see the test strip), as well as on a private right-of-way owned by the Long Island Motor Parkway Company, which was used as a race course for the William K. Vanderbilt, Jr., automobile cup race. This eleven-mile section, built in 1908 with super-elevated curves, was paved with steel-wire-mesh Hassam-type reinforced concrete, twenty-four feet wide, in two courses, with a total thickness of five inches. It was a prototype surface for the twentieth-century highway of the future.

Many old roads, given their various resurfacings over time, are ideal below-ground archaeological sites, a phenomenon that researchers working along the National Road in Ohio recently confirmed. A road's surface history also exists in most state highway offices, where a comprehensive road inventory is maintained for those highways for which the department is responsible. Appropriately called a "road life" profile, this inventory records every change that has occurred both to the road and the roadside since the department assumed its maintenance.

The serious landscape observer can also occasionally discover artifacts of the road's past life if

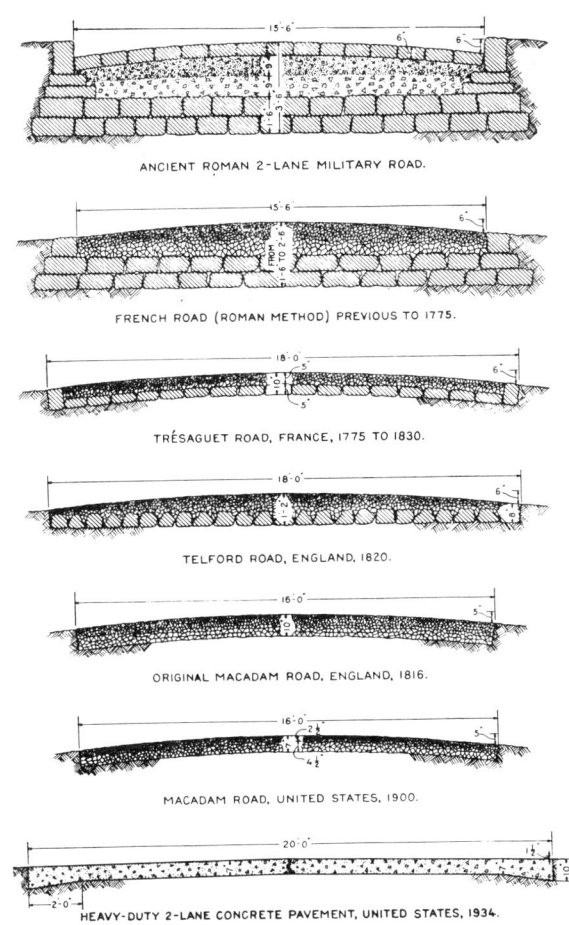

Fig. 17. Cross sections of roads from ancient to modern times. *Princeton University Press.*

he scrutinizes that surface with special attention. Thereon or therein, depending on how many layers of former roadbeds are exposed in mini-archaeological excavations (my euphemism for urban potholes) occurring annually during spring thaws and as a result of heavy traffic, are often found fragments of an area's urban transportation history. For example, in Indianapolis's Virginia Avenue, formerly a plank road, I came upon the remnants of cedar block pavers, parts of an interurban railroad line, a nineteenth-century macadam surface, and a twentieth-century concrete pavement.

Any road surface is full of historical surprises. Along Georgetown's streets in the District of Columbia one finds evidence of an array of past aesthetics in paving design as well as in paving materials: one discovers granite formed in arcs, brick laid in various bonds or herringbone patterns, and cobbles set in random ashlar fashion. In Holly Springs, Mississippi, the unique rounded bricks found embedded in many of its streets, sidewalks, and even the First Presbyterian Church betray the whimsey of early city dwellers, and also are a trademark of the area's local kilns. In Portland, Oregon, Friends of Pioneer Square have repaved one of their civic spaces with "special donor bricks," inscribing each with a philanthropic citizen's name. Indianapolis has similarly bricked its famous Circle and streets approaching it. In New Castle, Delaware, some of the streets and sidewalks have been paved with the stone ties once used on the now-defunct state railroad.

Probably one of the most unsung, yet most vital, components of the road is the lowly culvert, a highway engineering feature usually partially submerged under the roadbed and hence largely unnoticed. The term "culvert" encompasses practically all closed conduits used for highway drainage with the exception of storm drains. Like any artifact, culverts can be classified in a typology that includes pipe, pipe arch, box, bridge, or arch culverts. One of these types, the corrugated metal pipe culvert, is the 1896 invention of two Crawfordsville, Indiana, men—Stanley Simpson, the town engineer, and James H. Watson, a sheet metal worker. (See Fig. 19.) Their patented pipe culvert, first utilized when Union Township in Montgomery County installed two sixty-inch diameter pipes to replace a washed-out bridge across Crazy Creek, has now become a common sight on highway construction projects around the world.

Fig. 18. Dust suppression truck working on an unidentified southern Indiana road, ca. 1930. *Indiana State Highway Commission*.

Fig. 19. The First Corrugated Culvert Factory, Crawfordsville, Indiana, 1896. *Armco, Inc.*

With the advent of the automobile, still other new road features appeared along the highway, particularly in the form of traffic controls. The first pedestrian safety island appeared in San Francisco in 1907. The first painted center dividing line was used in Michigan and Wisconsin in 1911. The first one-way streets came long before the automobile. They were invented in Rome, in the time of Julius Caesar, in an effort to keep the chariots moving through the business district during the rush hours. New York passed its and the nation's first motor vehicle law in 1901. It required every automobile to display the initials of the owner in a conspicuous place. Owners had to make their own plates. By 1910, city traffic was in need of control, and the first traffic signal—a manually operated semaphore—appeared. Detroit worried about night drivers and hung colored lanterns on its semaphores for operation after dark. Cleveland's Euclid Avenue boasted the first electric traffic signal in 1904. It had red and green lights, with a warning buzzer as the color changed. The classic red-yellow-green stoplight as we know it today appeared in New York in 1918. Traffic continued to thicken, forcing the city of Buffalo to devise the "No Left Turn" in 1916.

Roads as Streets

When roads enter cities and towns, their names often change to include the term "street," a word partially derived from the Latin *sterne*, to pave. The first roads to be paved were indeed in cities. For example, in the remains of ancient Babylon archaeologists have found paved streets of burnt brick and stone set in mortar dating from 3,000 B.C.; and, as early as 1657, New York achieved the distinction of being the first city in North America, after European settlement, to pave one of its thoroughfares, naming it, if not imaginatively not inappropriately, Stone Street. The above-ground archaeologist, therefore, considers the street as an urban manifestation of the road. Since streets usually have a high concentration of artifactual evidence on, around, and even under them, they are exciting research sites and deserve careful scrutiny for what their physical environments can tell us about their builders and users.

To be able to understand streets as the historical museums that they are, we need to classify them by various typologies. One obvious research classification is simply what they are called or have been called. A current street name, for example, may tell the landscape observer where that street originally went or came from; hence, in Indianapolis, one finds Millersville Road, Allisonville Road, Pendleton Pike, Shelbyville Road, Madison Avenue, Crawfordsville Road,

Fig. 20. Traffic cop at the intersection of Virginia Avenue and Delaware and Maryland streets, Indianapolis, 1918. *Bass Photo*.

READING THE ROAD 31

Zionsville Road, and the Michigan (Northwestern Avenue) Road. Occasionally a street sign or road sign tells the landscape historian of a city's influence far beyond its boundaries, as happens when one comes upon the Little Chicago Road just outside of Indianapolis or the boulevard to Indianapolis just outside Chicago.

In his guide to *Street-Names of Philadelphia* (1975), Robert I. Alotta points out that the earliest recorded street names were usually derived from their point of destination. Next in abundance are street names derived from those individuals who once owned, subdivided, or sold the land that the streets now traverse. Here one thinks of Beale Street in Memphis, Olvera Street in Los Angeles, and Diversey Street in Chicago. Another major category of American street names is honorific, giving us a glimpse of those individuals whom previous town planners, real estate speculators, and city councils thought worthy of being commemorated for posterity by the stroke of putting their names on the map. While this practice varies from one region to another as it was applied to local heroes, there have been certain national trends in honorific street naming since the early nineteenth century. The revolutionary generation (especially Franklin, Washington, and Jefferson) enjoyed the first vogue, followed by a Lincolnmania and a celebration of Civil War heroes in late nineteenth-century America. Recent American history, particularly several of its more violent episodes (e.g., in the wake of the assassinations of President John F. Kennedy and civil-rights advocate Rev. Martin Luther King) produced a trend toward the renaming of American city streets and sites.

Often called Towne Streete when it was a single wilderness road in New England, High Street in New Jersey, Broad Street in Pennsylvania, Market Street in Ohio, Grand Street in Wyoming, and debunked by Sinclair Lewis's famous novel about its presence in Gopher Prairie, Minnesota, but celebrated by Walt Disney's theme parks, Main Street constitutes one of the most omnipresent artifacts of American history. So many main roads eventually become main streets that Carole Rifkind, in her pictorial history of *Main Street: The Face of Urban America* (1977), considers this urban road type as "the face and foundation of the United States."

Fifth, Madison, Park, and Pennsylvania avenues and Sunset, Wilshire, and Bruckner boulevards are still other names of interest to the above-ground archaeologist, not only for their local history in their places of origin but also for the progeny they have spawned elsewhere on the landscape. In addition to these famous American streets and their many imitators, there is also a history behind those dubbed "Strips" (e.g., in Las Vegas, Nevada), "Miracle Miles" (e.g., in Coral Gables, Florida), and "Broadways" (from the original Dutch, *Breede Wegh*). One even comes upon streets called only that—"The Street"—such as the main road running through the town of Deerfield, Massachusetts.

In addition to their names, streets should be studied as to their size: today's standard width of thirty-two feet (pre-1920 streets were usually twenty-six feet) was determined by motorized vehicular traffic instead of the numerous other factors in the past. An example: the width of many western main streets was sixty-six feet, which was the diameter of a circle in which a standard horse-and-wagon team could be turned around. Other factors to be considered are the street's shape (e.g., circular, elliptical, linear), its general usage (e.g., commercial, industrial, residential, recreational), and its specific economic function (e.g., for financial districts, automobile dealer rows, entertainment strips, vice districts). Whereas street size, shape, and original usage and function can help the present traveler trace the path of the road's (and its city's) history, one should never overlook obvious naming leads. For example, the location of a town's earlier economic base might be recorded in street names such as Dock, Front, Water, Levee, Wharf, Embarcadero,

Fig. 21. Alley in Charlottesville, Indiana, on U.S. 40 east of Greenfield, Indiana, 1983. *IHS—Seldon Bradley.*

Hydraulic, or Ferry. Where cities have back-filled their earlier shorelines or river banks, as in Boston, such so-named streets, although now considerably inland, survive to help the above-ground archaeologist document the town's original water boundary.

In constructing such a typology for the principal streets of a town or city, the landscape historian should not neglect the historical importance of little streets such as closes, mews, lanes, byways, and alleys. In two fascinating books, a general one on *Alleys: A Hidden Resource* (1978) by Grady Clay and a specific site study on *Alley Life of Washington* [D.C.] (1980) by James Borchert, we have valuable guides to the "streets" behind "the" street. As Clay remarks, "to skulk through an American alley is to step backward in time and to attempt to overcome the fact that the written history of architecture and town planning has a visual fix on frontality, a permanent obesssion 'en face.'" Unfortunately, since out of sight seems to mean out of the American mind, the residential alley has been the academic, geographic, and social outcast of the built environment for at least a half century. Likewise, the commercial and industrial alley has never been given its just due in the written history of American urban economic life. Alleys are considered wastelands, haunts of the unwanted, worlds of trash collectors, cats, week-end car mechanics, and children. They are places filled with garages, public utility conduits, water mains, telephone lines, sewers, and, as Borchert has shown, a wide range of housing stock for servants, the poor, and the transient. Yet alleys are fascinating above-ground archaeological sites. "More often than not," notes Grady Clay quoting Lewis Mumford, "I would prefer to walk in the rear alley, precisely for all those little hints of life, activity, and transition which the placid visual arts of suburbia did their best to suppress or politely disguise."

Like alleys, front streets, too, are cluttered with historical evidence that we all walk by (or sometimes directly on) everyday. I speak here of street surfaces, utilities, furnishings, and fixtures—a hodge-podge of familiar objects: traffic signals, fire hydrants, letter

Fig. 22. Christmas lighting along Wabash Avenue in Terre Haute, Indiana, 1960. *Martin Collection, IHS.*

boxes, gas mains, lamp posts, store fronts (ever-changing museums of American consumerism), telephone booths, manhole covers, civic fountains, public timepieces, and parking meters.

Constantly "looking down" to find such artifacts is one of the pedestrian (in both senses) but rewarding research strategies of the above-ground archaeologist. If we neglect to gaze downwards, we miss much history on the road. For example, consider the colophon that the authors, Carol Olwell and Judith Waldhorn, of *A Gift to the Street* (1976) chose for their book, a symbol of the anonymous builders of so many of San Francisco's vernacular houses: that is, the cast-iron circle within a square found embedded in the sidewalk in front of many of the city's homes. This iron grate, a fine example of above-ground archaeological evidence, served two purposes: it vented sewer gas and it advertised the early builders and suppliers who left at our feet a small signature of the nineteenth century. Those all-but-forgotten calling cards remain as their footprints, historical markers on which we often, quite unthinkingly, impress our own footprints as we pass them by.

Unless you trudge around city streets occasionally with your head down, you are also likely to miss valves that turn gas and water on and off, caps to fuel-oil lines, and openings to sewers, pipes, and other conduits that represent the Victorians' century-long effort to sanitize and civilize the urban street and its adjoining abodes. These artifacts also recall, when viewed in conjunction with other sidewalk elements (e.g., street elevators, dumb waiters, coal hatches, delivery chutes), the nineteenth-century trend, especially among owners of commercial buildings, to exercise "squatter's rights" (a practice with a long American history) out, on to, and under the public street in front of their structures.

Manhole covers, street openings large enough to accommodate human access, were discovered as an art object by artists and designers some years ago. Since then there have been photo exhibits, studies like Mimi and Richard Foley's *The Manhole Covers of Los Angeles* (1976), and even a book of rubbings dealing with this common yet largely unnoticed artifact. The format of the manhole cover appears to have partially inspired some contemporary art works that the above-ground archaeologist now finds inlaid in modern city sidewalks. In Seattle, for instance, you can tell exactly where you are in the city by means of any one of nineteen manhole covers that also act as urban road maps. Each displays a downtown street grid featuring such attractions as the Space Needle, Freeway Park, and the Pike Place Market, and each has a shiny, stainless steel marker embedded in the map pinpointing the cover's location in the city.

Street surface art appears in many other unsuspected places. Situated in the Haymarket, Boston's past and present outdoor market site near the Italian North End, the landscape historian comes upon Mags Harries's *Asaroton 1976*, a humorous collage of bronze replicas of the market's everyday debris (e.g., banana peels, waste paper, cabbage leaves) set into the crosswalk. Back in Seattle, appropriately along Broadway Street in the Capitol Hill area, we find Jack Mackie's *Dancer's Steps*—eight panels of bronze shoe soles arranged into dancing diagrams, with arrows explaining both traditional and modern dance patterns—embedded in the cement sidewalk as part of an urban improvement program.

Along Nassau Street in Princeton, New Jersey, I can come upon my professional counterpart in front of Borough Hall: a university professor, in the form of a realistic life-size bronze figure, comfortably settled on a park bench reading his *New York Times* with the 1974 headline, "Nixon Resigns." In Seattle, one finds two perennial bench sitters, "He and She," a pair of whimsical, anonymous, life-size folk characters created out of the oral tradition of a residential area called "the Regrade" which, ninety years ago, was under a large mound of earth called Denny's Hill. As steely office buildings and condominiums now replace the sporadic empty lots and vernacular architecture of the former community, these three-dimensional denizens of the road, created by artist Howard Garnitz, remain fixed witnesses to the metamorphosis of the neighborhood.

The blue-collar, "gritty city" of Chelsea, Massachusetts, tells similar stories via its street furniture and small-scale public art. Small bronze crabs embedded in the brick pavement of the city's public square remind observant pedestrians that seafood was sold here half a century ago. A grouping of life-size bronze figures depicting contemporary residents in conversation gives human scale to the refurbished square, while other bronze sculpture objects remind us of life's small encounters: a shopping bag sits near a public telephone, a handbag rests on the bus stop bench, a half-eaten lunch remains on a bollard, a sweater lies on the pavement.

From the nineteenth century onwards, city streets witnessed not only the multiplication of forms of street transport and street furniture, but also expanded activities to drain, light, police, regulate, and ornament those streets and their adjoining buildings. American municipalities experimented with various sources to illuminate their urban thoroughfares, but natural gas, then electricity, triumphed in what historian Kate

Bolton, writing in 1979 in the journal *Landscape*, has called "the great awakening of the night." As early as 1817, Baltimore had installed gaslights on one of its city streets, and original examples of such city lights can still be found in the Clifton neighborhood of Cincinnati. In addition to spawning numerous evening entertainment areas (e.g., Gaslight Square in St. Louis, Old Town in Chicago), the gaslit era of American urban history migrated to our suburbs, where any number of eternal flames (since it was once considered cheaper to let the gas jet burn continually day and night) were installed in the 1860s.

The electrification of city streets, beginning in the 1880s, produced even more marked changes in road life than had gaslighting. In her study of *Public Street Illumination in Washington, D.C.: An Illustrated History* (1975), Sarah Noreen has established a beginning typology for investigating such material culture. Her volume serves as a basic primer for identifying American street and road lighting and for interpreting the role it has played in the economic, cultural, aesthetic, recreational, and even racial history of American cities. Street lights can tell us, for example, about a bit of local history, as do those in New Orleans or Salt Lake City, where we find events of those communities' pasts commemorated in reliefs on the light standards. Street lights can sometimes alert us to the boundaries between municipalities, as does the change in lamp posts marking the otherwise unnoticed border between the suburban communities of Evanston and Wilmette north of Chicago.

Large-scale urban timepieces are other historical markers of past city street life. Predecessor of the mechanical clock, the sundial of antiquity is now only rarely found in city squares and on building facades (Fig. 23). The public clock of the pre-twentieth-century urban environment also seems to be disappearing from the landscape in some type of inverse ratio to the number of private, personal watches with which we have increasingly adorned ourselves. Public clocks recall an earlier pace of city life, a time when more citizens were cognizant of communal time and less equipped with personal timepieces to keep track of their own individual time. The proliferation of public clocks in the industrial city—on railroad stations, at business corners, atop commercial offices, on the facades of civic structures—dramatized, much like the factory whistle, our increasing fascination with harnessing, measuring, and controlling time in so many facets of modern life. This inordinant consciousness of proximate time, of course, continues, but it is now manifested in the artifacts of the digital revolution (Fig. 24). Fortunately, some public clocks still survive in many American cities as mechanical fossils of an age when local boosters (particularly jewelers, bankers, and merchandisers) saw an obvious way to combine self-interest with social altruism in their civic philanthropy. Sometimes one city's entrepreneur sets out to ape another, and thus the above-ground archaeologist who shops at Marshall Field's department store in Chicago notes the striking similarity of its famous 1904 corner clock to the large timepiece that he or she will find on the L. S. Ayres store along U.S. 40's Washington Street in Indianapolis (Fig. 25).

What we find along urban streets can tell us much about local commercial rivalries, changing aesthetic sensibilities, and cultural aspirations. We can also learn what communities have valued in their own history. Such attitudes can be analyzed from the public sculpture (Fig. 26), fountains, civic art, and historical monuments extant along any roadscape.

The advent of the automobile has greatly affected the size, placement, and type of such street and road furnishings as well as the facilities necessary for the vehicle itself. The first parking lots date from the mid-1920s and parking meters first appeared on the streets of Oklahoma City and Tulsa, Oklahoma, by the mid-1930s. In *I Hear America Talking* (1976), Stuart Berg Flexner dates the usage of the term parking garage to 1924, the filling station to 1915, and the service station

Fig. 23. Sundial on the Indiana Repertory Theatre on West Washington Street (U.S. 40) in Indianapolis, 1983. *IHS—Seldon Bradley.*

to 1922. In 1918, a used-car lot in Chicago started renting out twelve vehicles to drivers, thus becoming the country's first car-rental firm. That lot was bought in 1923 by John D. Hertz, president of the Yellow Cab Company of Chicago, who renamed the fledgling operation The Hertz Drive-U-Self System.

Roads as Strips

In analyzing the American road, the above-ground archaeologist cannot avoid a type of thoroughfare called the "Strip." Although we normally think of this landscape feature as a result of universal car ownership in the twentieth century, its origins lie in a road pattern that Grady Clay has called "River Strips" and in the commercial ribbon development spawned in the streetcar era of the late nineteenth century. (See Fig. 27.) The widespread adoption of the automobile in America simply accelerated a land-use process already at work: wherever cheap land was readily accessible, commercial functions began to extend, in linear fashion, out along urban arteries. More recently, the process has also tended to focus on the cheap, available land around newly built interstate exchanges.

Fig. 24. Digital time and temperature clock on the Merchants National Bank Building at the southeast corner of Meridian and Washington (U.S. 40) streets in Indianapolis, 1984. *IHS—Seldon Bradley.*

A commercial strip, to isolate its usual qualities, has to be on a heavily traveled street or road. As a twentieth-century landscape artifact, it is usually defined by geographers as a noncentral business area of commercial activity, of linear configuration, wherein a road or highway is lined by primarily retail establishments whose clientele are largely automobile-borne customers. Thus the strip invariably requires direct car access and parking.

The commercial strip, variously referred to as the "suburban ribbon," "neon strip," "commercial ribbon," "string street," or simply "the Strip," generally consists of cheaply built one-story structures and ex-

Fig. 25. Clock on L.S. Ayres and Company, an Indianapolis department store, at the southwest corner of Meridian and Washington (U.S. 40) streets in Indianapolis, 1981. *Indianapolis Star-News.*

travagant signs. While many of these structures appear, at first glance, to be visually bland containers, the above-ground archaeologist recognizes that their expressive adornment, their symbolic configuration, and their architectural signage merit a closer look—particularly if he is interested in the historical roots of contemporary American culture. Geographer Barry Gordon, analyzing "The Commercial Strip as an Indicator of American Cultural Themes" (M.A. thesis, 1972), suggests several major characteristics of strip material culture that we might examine in attempting to understand this road type: 1) competitive self-interest and excessive privatism (lavish attention on lighting and commercial signage and little regard for the public road or its edge); 2) a high rate of rapid consumption of resources and concomitant creation of waste (solid, liquid, and gaseous); 3) impermanence (incessant external remodeling of signs, facades, even the entire shapes of buildings, not for structural but for advertising reasons).

The commercial strip is a difficult road feature to comprehend because it is such a mercurial, sprawling, often seemingly banal, melange of constant activity, colorful light (especially at night), and popular culture. However, in Robert Venturi's provocative book, *Learning from Las Vegas* (1977), we have a model above-ground archaeological study of the strip in its most famous setting. Venturi points out that, in addition to being a huge collective work of pop art, there is no place on the North American continent that so powerfully symbolizes the American Dream of unending motion, unrestrained competition, and free enterprise as the strip. While Las Vegas is but our best example of the highway strip civilization, the above-ground archaeologist also discovers similar sites on Ventura Boulevard in Los Angeles; Broadway Street in Minneapolis; Colfax Avenue in Denver; the Warsaw-Glenway corridor in Cincinnati; Coralville Road outside Iowa City, Iowa; Erie Boulevard in Syracuse; or University Avenue in Champaign-Urbana, Illinois.

Fig. 26. Statue of Thomas A. Hendricks, governor of Indiana (1873-77) and vice-president of the United States (1885), on the southeast corner of the grounds of the Indiana State Capitol on Washington Street (U.S. 40), in Indianapolis, 1984. *IHS—Seldon Bradley.*

The case of the Champaign-Urbana commercial strip has suggested to geographer John Jakle a five-stage model of strip history applicable to other such above-ground archaeological sites in the United States. In a study of "The Evolution of a Commercial Strip" (*Journal of Cultural Geography*, 1981), Jakle and

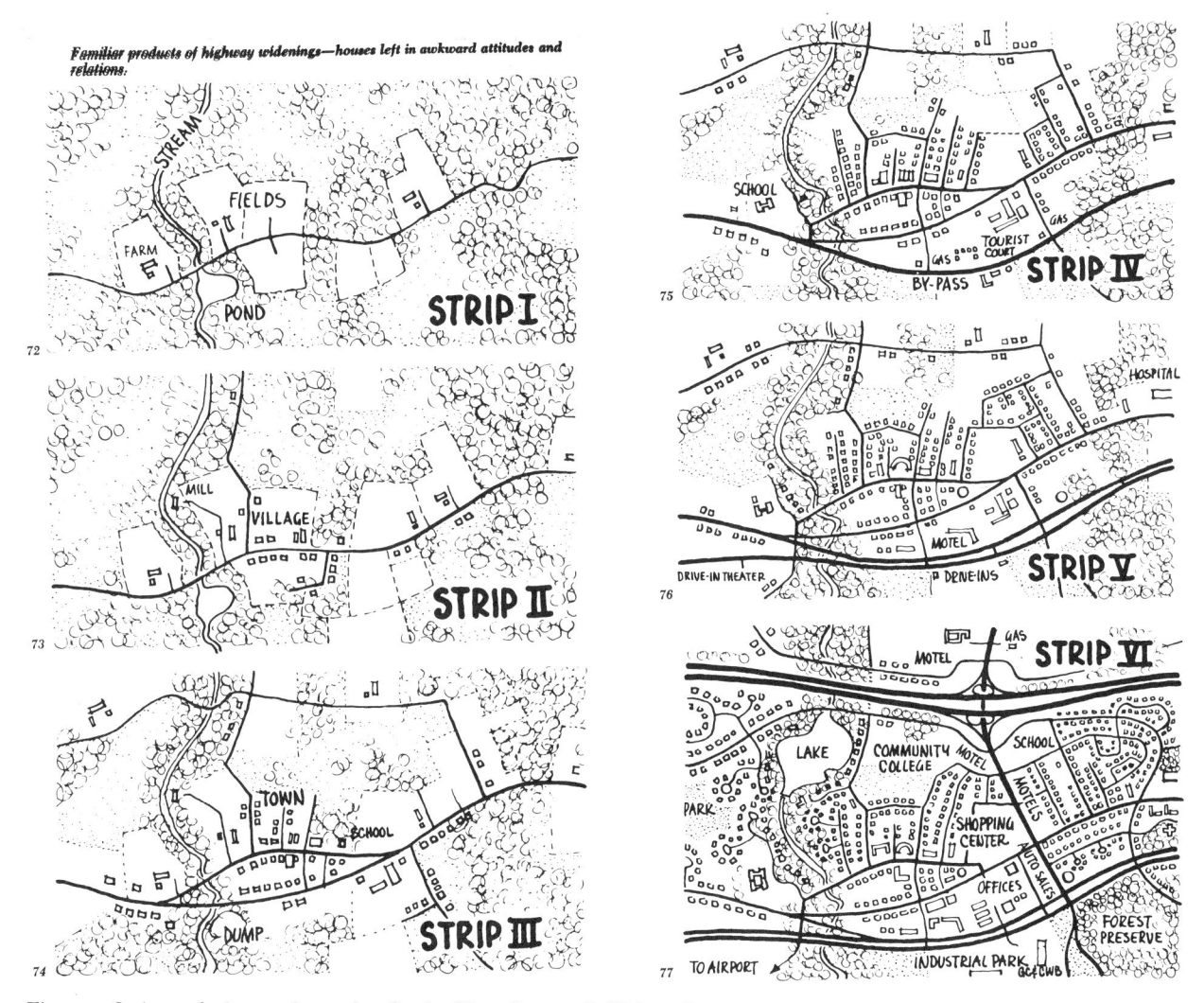

Fig. 27. Strip evolution as drawn by Grady Clay. *Praeger Publishers, Inc.*

coauthor Richard L. Mattson claim we should think of the historical development of the strip in terms of collective and individual decision making, whereby private and public interests shape a linear space devoted primarily to commerce. Previously such a space may have been given to agricultural, residential, or other land use. Jakle's model deals with the conversion of a residential street, University Avenue, into a typical commercial strip that the above-ground archaeologist might find on the outskirts of any urban complex, anywhere in the country. Of course, strips also evolve from other land use patterns, particularly terrain once devoted to argriculture or previously ignored because of its marginal economic value.

In Jakle's proposed morphology, a stable residential street comprised primarily of single-family dwellings

40 U.S. 40: A ROADSCAPE OF THE AMERICAN EXPERIENCE

constitutes Stage One. A few neighborhood businesses are oriented to pedestrian traffic and do not detract from the quiescent quality of a predominantly residential thoroughfare.

In Stage Two, gasoline stations form the vanguard of an intrusive commercial development. These stations serve traffic moving to and from a nearby central business district. They are located primarily on previously vacant corner lots. Investments in buildings and driveways are modest, and these businesses have an impermanent, transient look.

Gasoline station development continues in Stage Three, where it reaches a peak. Indeed, descriptions such as "gasoline alley" or "gasoline row" might be applied to the road at this point in its evolution. However, the addition of other business types brings greater commercial diversity to the street. Except where commercial establishments are located in the middle of blocks, residences and businesses still coexist in relative stability. Although the number of domestic dwellings declines, the number of residents remains much the same, as more buildings are divided into multiple units. Fewer landlords live in their buildings.

Commercial functions clearly dominate in Stage Four. A significantly larger number and wider variety of businesses characterize the street. Largely because of competition, gasoline stations decline numerically, resulting in the remaining stations being more evenly distributed in the linear array. Especially evident in Stage Four is the growth of the automobile-convenient establishments, such as drive-in restaurants and motels with off-street parking facilities. The size of business lots increases, due in part to the necessity of providing parking lots. Business buildings do tend to be larger, however, and better constructed, and a sense of commercial permanence pervades the thoroughfare. Street widening and the removal of trees substantially alter the street's personality. The number of residences declines sharply, while the number of vacant dwellings increases. Income levels of residents along the street fall substantially, and multiple-unit rental housing owned by absentee landlords prevails.

In Stage Five, residential functions along the street all but disappear. Only a few relic rental units survive in what is otherwise a totally commercial landscape. Commercial properties increase in size as more businesses provide off-street parking and expand their layouts to accommodate the growing number of customers. Huge billboards and colossal signs come to dominate the visual landscape in a profusion of commercial advertising, light, and color.

The commercial strip's billboards—an early twentieth-century roadside extension of the large wall advertisements once painted on the side facades of nineteenth-century urban structures—are often larger than the buildings that they advertise. Such billboards and signs remind the above-ground archaeologist of the triumphal arches erected by the ancient Romans, a civilization to which contemporary Americans are often compared and a culture especially known for its road system. As Robert Venturi has noted, the series of arches that once lined the highways leading into Rome are but prototypes of the twentieth-century highway billboards, with necessary changes having been made for scale, speed, and content.

The triumphal arches in Rome were primarily spatial markers, channeling the flow of ceremonial processions through a complex urban landscape. Uniformly spaced and strategically placed, they were intentionally designed to convey important messages to the populace. On Route U.S. 40 along commercial strips outside the cities of Terre Haute or Richmond, one finds contemporary billboards, in a series, set at a constant angle toward the oncoming traffic, that serve a function not unlike the arches along the Via Appia. They mark our way, if not to the ancient forum or pantheon, then to less regal emporiums called Caesar's Palace or Noble Roman's.

Fig. 28. Commercial corner at the intersection of Central Avenue and 25th streets in Indianapolis, ca. 1940. *IHS*.

Contemporary signage on the modern commercial strip is a riot of mixed media—words, pictures, and sculpture—all intended to attract, inform, persuade, and entice us to leave the road for the roadside. Many road signs hawk their messages both day and night. The same sign works as a polychromatic sculpture in the sun and as a black silhouette against the sky; at night it is a source of illumination. Often it revolves by day and becomes a dance of lights at night. Where possible, the modern commercial strip sign aspires to be a superlative. For example, Las Vegas claims the longest sign in the world (the Thunderbird), and the highest (the Dunes). The sign of the city's Pioneer Club, a cowboy giant sixty-feet high, even talks, saying "Howdy Pardner" every sixty seconds.

To comprehend such mammoth and increasingly omnipresent artifacts along the road, Tom Wolfe recommends that the landscape historian devise a new nomenclature to classify and study such modern material culture. "They soar in shapes before which the existing vocabulary of art history is helpless," confesses the author of *The Kandy-Kolored Tangerine-Flake Streamline Baby* (1966). "I can only attempt to supply names—Boomerang Modern, Palette Curvilinear, Flash Gordon Ming-Alert Spiral, McDonald's Hamburger Parabola, Mint Casino Elliptical, Miami Beach Kidney."

Road Artifacts I: Fuel, Food, Fun

Part of the exciting adventure of applying an aboveground archaeological perspective to the American highway is that one must develop new terminologies, research strategies, and new interpretive models. Such research can be pursued alone or in concert with other like-minded investigators interested in the idea of deciphering the contemporary roadscape as an outdoor museum of American culture. One such group has banded together in an organization called the Society for Commercial Archaeology. The society was founded in 1976 to promote the understanding, documentation, and preservation of significant structures and symbols of the commercial-built environment. Founder Chester Liebs, an architectural historian at the University of Vermont, says of the group's work: "We're trying to use the buildings rather than just the

Fig. 29. Commercial strip on U.S. 40 in Richmond, Indiana, 1983. *IHS—Seldon Bradley.* The picture was taken with a telephoto lens.

written record to understand a period—an approach used by archaeologists."

Understandably, these students of the twentieth-century landscape have been very interested in an American artifact called, over its history, the bulk station, the filling station, the lubritorium, the service station, or, simply, the gas station. As the first structure built in response to the automobile, the gas station, after the food store, is probably the most widespread type of commercial building in America. Moreover, since the gas station often established design solutions and aesthetic trends that became standard for many other types of highway architecture, the above-ground archaeologist should master its architectural history as one reference guide by which to interpret other material culture of the "motorscape" that so pervades the contemporary American landscape. Fortunately, many communities still contain an instructive array of stations that enable one to trace the station's numerous transformations, functional developments, and various cultural meanings over the span of three-quarters of a century. To assist in this field research, one might consult Daniel Vieyra's *"Fill'er Up": An Architectural History of America's Gas Station*

READING THE ROAD 43

(1979). Fig. 30 details the key features of a typology that one might also use to locate stations along a chronology from 1910 through 1970.

Semipublic facilities for storing and servicing automobiles had been operating in New York and other eastern cities since the turn of the century. They were often located in blacksmith shops, bicycle stores, and liveries. Historian James Flink, in *America Adopts the Automobile, 1895-1910* (1970), credits Seattle with the establishment of the first truly public gasoline station and St. Louis with the development of the first station chain (the American Gasoline Company) in 1907. This first generation of stations was comprised of either adaptations of existing stores with the addition of pumps (often placed in the structure's interior), or they were modeled on the one-story residential bungalow with a pitched roof. In recent years, we have witnessed a return to this early residential scale and styling in structures like Shell's "ranch house" and Sunoco's and Gulf's "universal colonial suburban." In between these two stylistic trends, the Residential Eclectic of 1910-1920 and the Residential Suburban of 1960-1980 are at least two other dominant architectural vocabularies. The above-ground archaeologist will easily recognize the 1930s' streamlined, curvilinear expanses of porcelain and glass Art Moderne which was followed by the clean geometry of the International (German Bauhaus) Style, using flat roofs, glass facades, right-angled corner windows, and smooth horizontal lines—all features appropriate to the rectilinear plan of the prefabricated service garage, popular after World War II.

Such architectural definition was achieved as the filling station assumed the role of product advertising for national oil companies such as Gulf Oil, which pioneered in station franchising as early as 1913. Standardized and distributed across the country, extant franchise stations can be interpreted as a sophisticated reflection of American ideals as viewed and promulgated by the nation's oil oligarchies. In contrast, local oil companies, independent entrepreneurs, and discount stations often proclaimed their highway identity and independence from such corporate assimilation by idiosyncratic pop-art structures bedecked in brilliant colors, extravagant imagery, soaring arches, and flying cantilevers designed to catch the motorist's eye. These exuberant statements by owners who did not want their stations to blend in, conform, or be too sleek are an above-ground archaeologist's delight. As unbridled expressions of individuality, they belong to the first half of this century, when there were few interstates and uniformity did not threaten to dominate the roadside.

We also need to examine the design, style, size, geographical placement, and impact of those artifacts that shelter and service our road vehicles at their birth (e.g., automobile show rooms and new car dealer lots, Fig. 35), during their life (e.g., special service centers and parking facilities), and after their death (e.g., junkyards and parts salvage stores, Fig. 36). In addition to these typical structures of our pervasive car culture, the roadside is littered with numerous other auto shelters and service facilities: body repair shops, car washes and waxes, paint refinishers, transmission experts, customizing emporiums, rustproofing specialists, front-end and rear-end centers, brake clinics, not to mention brake shops, tire shops, upholstery shops, valve shops, ignition shops, and muffler shops.

The pre-interstate highway also sported many more diners (Figs. 37, 38), another distinctive artifact of the country's commercial archaeology now rapidly disappearing along with local roadhouses, barbecues, and other drive-in emporiums that once served up much of the nation's road food. Although the exact beginning of the American diner is uncertain, many think its originator may have been Walter Scott of Providence, Rhode Island, who began serving sandwiches, coffee, and pie off a horse-drawn wagon in 1872. For students of this durable artifact in the Northeast, researchers in the Society for Commercial Archaeology have pub-

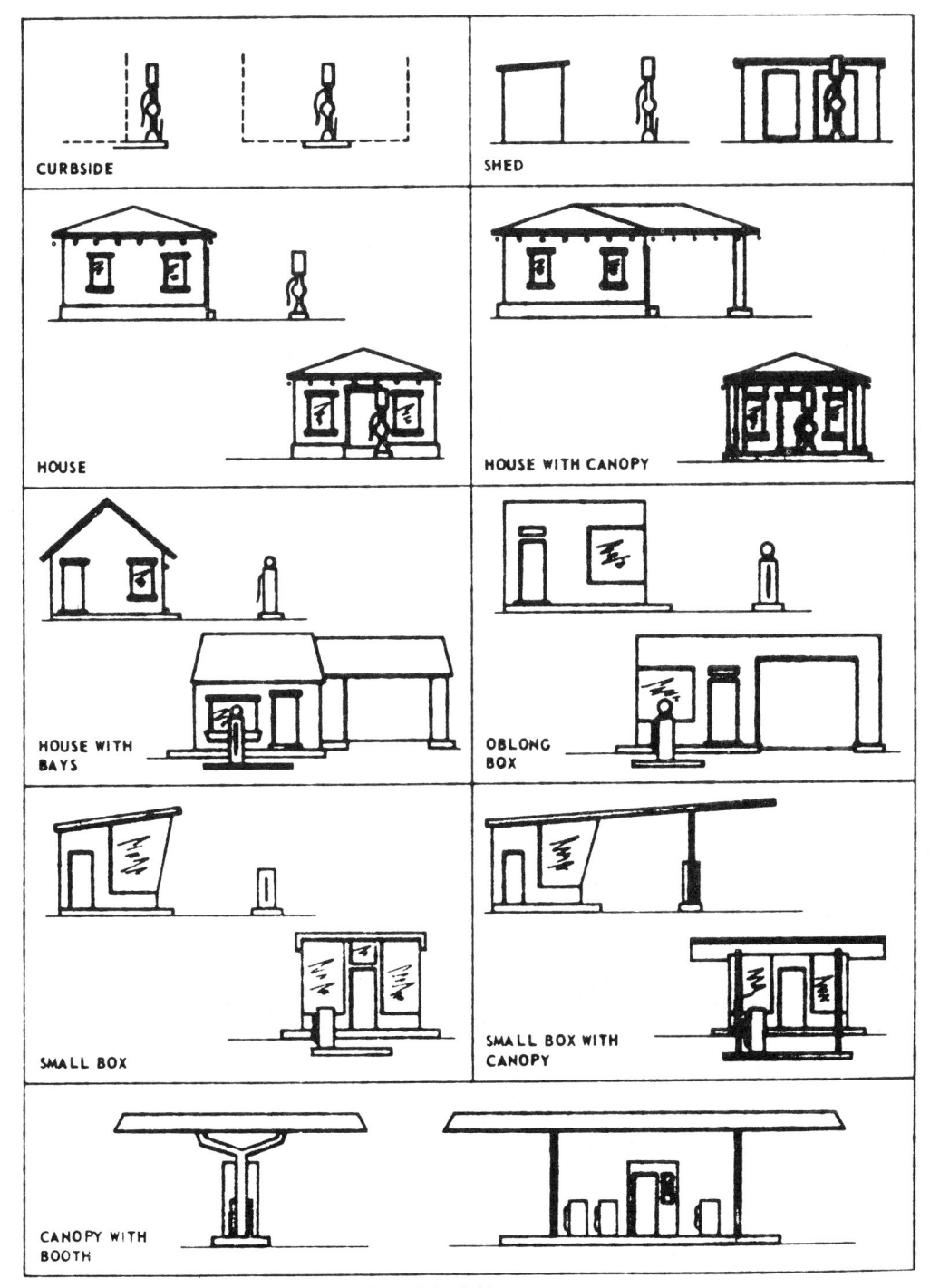

Fig. 30. Evolution of the gasoline station. *John Jakle*.

Fig. 31. Sinclair gasoline station on U.S. 31 near Walesboro in Bartholomew County, Indiana, ca. 1930. *Indiana Highway Commission.*

Fig. 32. Diamond Service Station at the intersection of U.S. 41 and Indiana 67 in Knox County, ca. 1930. *Indiana State Highway Commission.*

46   U.S. 40: A ROADSCAPE OF THE AMERICAN EXPERIENCE

Fig. 33. A first-generation gas station—the addition of pumps to an existing store—no longer pumping gas in Plainfield, Indiana, 1983. *IHS—Seldon Bradley.*

Fig. 34. Standard service station, the oblong box, on U.S. 40 in Knightstown, Indiana, 1981. *IHS—Seldon Bradley.*

READING THE ROAD 47

Fig. 35. New car dealership on East Washington Street in Indianapolis, 1983. *IHS—Seldon Bradley.*

Fig. 36. G. W. Pierce auto junkyard on U.S. 40 between Greenfield and Knightstown, Indiana, 1983. *IHS—Seldon Bradley.*

Figs. 37 and 38. Exterior and interior of the Downey Dunker restaurant, on North Pennsylvania Street in Indianapolis, ca. 1950. *Bretzman Collection, IHS.*

lished an *All-Night Diner Tour* (1980) identifying typical examples in the cities of Providence (where it is often claimed that the diner was born), Worcester (an early manufacturing center of diner units), and Boston (a center of great diner popularity).

When they first appeared in large numbers in the 1920s, drive-in restaurants, like gasoline stations and diners, employed exotic and glamorous versions of historical styles and fantasy in their architecture. And if the East Coast remains the best outdoor museum of the diner, then the West Coast is the premier aboveground archaeological site for what David Gebhard, Jim Heimann, and Rip Georges aptly call "California Crazy" roadside vernacular architecture. In their 1980 book of that title, this trio of commercial archaeologists catalogue a visual riot of short-order establishments that present themselves in buildings shaped like their products or a related shape—chuck wagons, root-beer barrels, donuts, milk bottles, teapots, chili bowls, and even hot-dog-shaped hot-dog stands. This delightful architectural zaniness of the 1920s and 1930s, of course, is also in evidence all over the country: north—the Orange Julip in Plattsburgh, New York, Rt. 9; south—Mammy's Cupboard in Natchez, Mississippi, on Old Highway 61; and midwest—the Frank-N-Stein Restaurant, 4619 E. Dunes Highway, Gary, Indiana. The Coffee Pot near Cambridge City, Indiana (Fig. 39), is a marvelous U.S. 40 example. Are not these artifacts full-blown examples of pop art, appearing on the American landscape a full half-century before Andy Warhol ever created an oversize Campbell's soup can or Claes Oldenburg cooked up a cloth-and-vinyl cheeseburger?

Such commercial archaeology, like other landscape features of our drive-in culture, tells us much about ourselves. Do we not prefer convenience food which is relatively inexpensive, quickly prepared, and rapidly served to be eaten on the run? Are we not often determined to simplify as much of the distribution side of life as possible, and hence willing to patronize (the typical American eats an average of one out of every three meals outside the home) an informal, "fast-food" environment that promotes such mobility? Do we not take a certain delight in efficient service, clever packaging, and flow technology? The highway restaurant, be it a White Tower or a White Castle, a Howard Johnson or a Colonel Sanders, operates on these cultural preferences as well as promulgates them. How else do we explain McDonald's, an empire that has expanded from a single store in 1955 in Des Plaines, Illinois (now on the National Register of Historic Places, Fig. 40), to forty-five hundred eateries.

As we travel on the road celebrated by American writers from Walt Whitman to Jack Kerouac, food and fuel are necessities. Fun is, as well, if we are to believe the extant material culture of roadside museums, gift shops, amusements, zoos, movies, and tourist attractions that draw their life and livelihood from the concrete umbilical cords that crisscross the land. Since their economic enterprises are often so highly competitive, many roadside entrepreneurs must try all the harder to make us stop. They often do so through a seemingly endless series of billboards along the roadside.

Billboards have been enticing gullible travelers to places claiming to have "The World's Largest" Iron Man, Concrete Buffalo, City Block, Cheese, Ball of Twine, or Main Street, since Americans first took to the highways. Reptile Gardens in Rapid City (South Dakota), Rock City in Chattanooga (Tennessee), Wall Drug in Wall (South Dakota), Gatorland in St. Augustine (Florida), and Pioneer Village in Minden (Nebraska)—they all make a sideshow of the open road. *Amazing America* (1977) by Jane and Michael Stern is one above-ground archaeologist's guide to this highway vaudeville of the past. Quite naturally, along the American roadside we also come upon hundreds of museums devoted to the automobile, the artifact that spawned the car culture. These museums range, for example, along U.S. 40 from Charles Ellis's old one-

Fig. 39. The Coffee Pot on U.S. 40 near Cambridge City, Indiana, 1984. *IHS—Seth Rossman.*

bay gas station (filled with filling station memorabilia) in Stilesville, Indiana, to Terre Haute's Early Motor Museum on the city's Wabash Avenue. Occasionally car buffs have parodied their own automania, as in the roadside displays at Lemon Grove (Edsel Park) in Pennsylvania and at The Cadillac Ranch on Interstate 40 (formerly Route 66), five miles west of Amarillo, Texas (Fig. 41). The Cadillac Ranch is ten Cadillacs ranging from a 1949 fast-back coupé to a 1960 Sedan de Ville, all buried face down in a row and providing the student of the artifact with a monumental example of seriation and an informal history of the tail fin from its modest induction in the 1940s through the flaring 1950s to fins farewell by the 1960s. Created by a group known as Ant Farm, the ten "Caddies" emerge from the Texas earth like a great Detroit bumper crop, and

READING THE ROAD 51

Fig. 40. The first McDonald's in Des Plaines, Illinois, ca. 1960. *McDonald's.*

Fig. 41. Cadillac Ranch on Interstate 40, west of Amarillo, Texas. *McSpadden Photography.*

Fig. 42. The Corral Drive-in Theatre on U.S. 40 in Seeleyville, Indiana, 1983. *IHS—Seldon Bradley.*

are the only visual point of reference across the otherwise flat Panhandle.

Ant Farm's metal monoliths diagonally arched into the Texas sky remind the landscape historian of another vertical monument to roadside amusement—the drive-in movie complexes now abandoned along so many highways. Appropriately enough, drive-in theaters were conceived in 1933 in Camden, New Jersey, by two men selling automobile products. Their sales meeting became so crowded that they decided to show their promotional film outdoors in a parking lot, and an American institution was born. To the landscape watcher, drive-in movies are often one of the first indications of civilization in the transition from rural to urban space. Usually located between towns along commercial strips, they help define town borders. This mediating location served many purposes: the movie could draw on the population of the two towns; the land was cheaper; and neither town could be held responsible for what was often considered a sleazy place, an environment that supposedly changed the sexual behavior of America's youth. For example, there's a drive-in on the border between Panama City and Springfield, Florida, called the "Isle of View" (say it fast).

The typical drive-in movie of the 1950s consisted of a huge billboard screen, a projection bunker containing an office and snack bar, and a huge parking lot. In his study of *The End of the Road: Vanishing Highway Architecture in America* (1977), John Margolies has researched how many drive-in owners, in order to attract attention to their establishments, decorated, often in neon and bright pastels, the backs of their screens which faced the road.

Road Artifacts II: Shelters, Shops, Services

The tourist home, motor hotel, motor court, and the motel (a word fashioned from combining motor and hotel), like the drive-in movie and the fast-food franchise, are American innovations on the twentieth-century roadscape. Places to put up for the night have always been needed by Americans on the move: taverns, inns, coaching stations, and, by the nineteenth century, hotels of all types of economies and edifices have welcomed the American traveler. The automobile gave a new adventure to the national *Wanderlust* as touring became a part of traveling. Warren Belasco's survey of *Americans on the Road* (1979) is a basic text in understanding the evolving roadside and its homes away from home. From the auto-camping of the 1910s, an inexpensive, individualistic sport with somewhat "gypsy" implications, to the development of the "Kleen and Kozy Kabins" of the 1920s, to the motor court and motor inn of the 1930s, we have evidence of a changing motel morphology. This was vastly accelerated by the revised tax code of 1954 and the Highway Act of 1956 which promoted the development of new, multistory structures best-called highway hotels.

The evolution of the American motel from its origins in the vernacular architecture of the auto and cabin camp is depicted in Fig. 43, and the artifact's dominant variations in spatial organization and land use are summarized in Fig. 44. The alert above-ground archaeologist can still occasionally spot these varied places where Americans were wont to spend a night. For example, the establishment claiming to be the first (1925) to use the name motel—James Vail's Motel Inn, alongside Highway 101 in San Luis Obispo, California, still houses guests under the architectural persona of a Spanish Mission along the old El Camino Real. Frank Redford's recently restored Wigwam Village in Rialto, California, also recalls a type of regional historicism and romantic escapism. Perhaps the apex of this popular culture is the Madonna Inn at 100 Madonna Road in San Luis Obispo, built by, you guessed it, Alex Madonna (Fig. 45). A worthy competitor to the excesses of William Randolph Hearst's San Simeon just to its north, Madonna designed every one of his sumptuous guest rooms differently, many of them working off historical themes. Some rooms look like college dormitories, others like Tahitian swimming holes. A series of three road rooms is called Ren-dez-vous. Some bathrooms are grottos with spectacular waterfall toilets and sinks, and the inn is famous for its public waterfall urinals. Architect Charles Moore has described the motel as "one of the most surprising and surprisely-full experiences to be found along an American highway."

The Madonna Inn is just the opposite of the Holiday Inn philosophy ("The best surprise is no surprise") of standardized facilities which, as a cultural trend in the motel industry, began to evolve as early as 1940, when a group of Southern motel owners got together and founded Quality Courts. The first Holiday Inn opened in Memphis, Tennessee, in 1953, the brainstorm of Kemmons Wilson, who took his motel's name (and the idea for a motel sign as movie marquee shaped like a neon tropical palm) from a 1942 Bing Crosby and Fred Astaire movie of the same title. Life imitates art? Other giants of the contemporary motel industry, anxious to catch the harried motorist's eye, have also used traditional architectural forms as advertising. Northeastern resort area motels looked like Georgian town houses; southwestern motels remained loyal to Spanish haciendas. Ramada Inn capitalized on the familiar Williamsburg motif, Howard Johnson on the New England church.

Some historians may scoff at the American highway and its artifacts as a source of historical study, but to anyone interested in probing the attitudes of the typical contemporary American, who now changes his address every five years and drives more than ten thousand miles annually, the omnipresence of gasoline stations, motels, and drive-ins of all types looms as a significant cultural phenomenon. Should we not, therefore, give serious attention to identifying and interpreting (perhaps even collecting) the pluralistic, eclectic, vernacular, and regional—sometimes tediously similar, but other times refreshingly idiosyncratic—manifestations of the car culture spawned by the automobile highway?

Should we not try to understand the origins, placement, and meaning of the shopping center, another road institution established by Americans on the

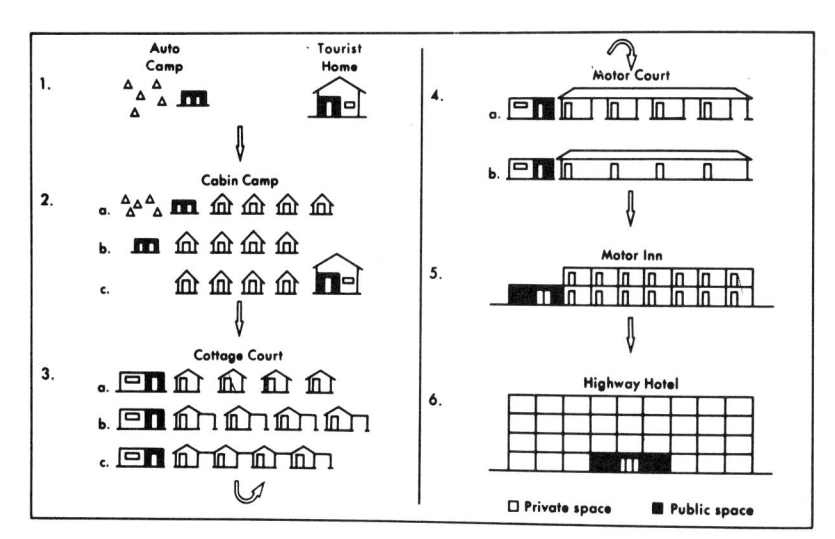

Fig. 43. The evolution of the American motel as a building type. *John Jakle.*

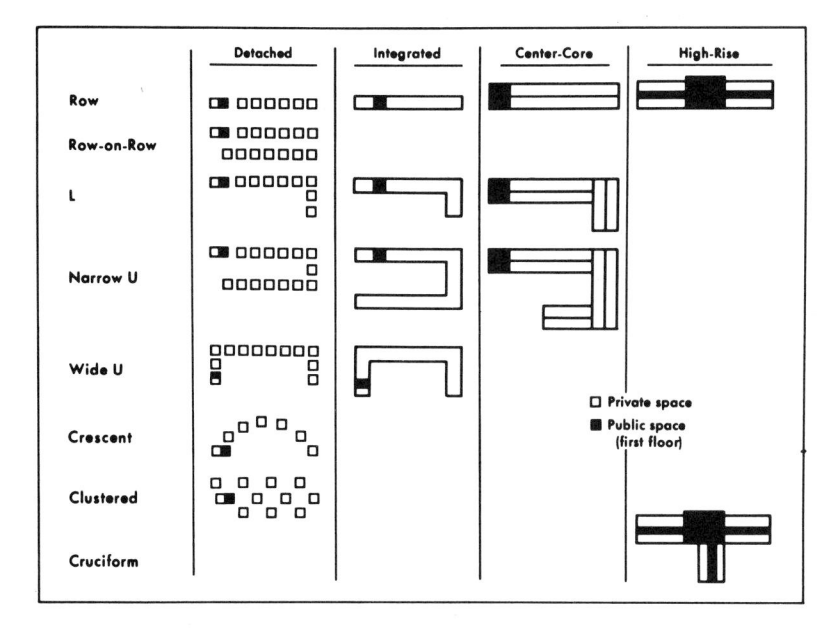

Fig. 44. Dominant variations in motel spatial organization. *John Jakle.*

READING THE ROAD 55

Fig. 45. The Madonna Inn at 100 Madonna Road in San Luis Obispo, California, ca. 1980. *The Madonna Inn*.

move? To begin to do so, the above-ground archaeologist can do no better than go to the source, in this case, the Country Club Plaza at 4629 Wornall Road in Kansas City (Missouri), where, in 1922, Jesse C. Nichols constructed the first large shopping center in the United States and the world. Nichols, a Kansas farm boy who, after graduating from the University of Kansas, took a graduate degree from Harvard, where he wrote a thesis on the economics of land development, then traveled abroad, visiting the English "Garden City" developments and Europe's architectural monuments. He returned home to apply what he had learned in creating a shopping center complex that now is host to one hundred and fifty stores, publishes its own newspaper (*The Plaza Bulletin*), and covers six thousand acres, which is approximately one-tenth of the whole area of downtown Kansas City (Figs. 46 and 47).

Shopping centers quickly became a new building type. By 1940, about one-fourth of the nation's retail-trade volume in metropolitan regions was dispersed into suburban shopping centers; by 1950 the amount was about one-third, and the percentage has increased with the decades. By 1955, some eighteen hundred shopping centers had been built outside metropolitan regions, calling themselves shopping malls, shopping complexes, and even shopping cities. The Woodfield Mall on Rt. 90 in Schaumburg, Illinois, presently rates as the world's largest shopping center. It is almost twice the size of Vatican City. On a good day its population exceeds two hundred thousand, and there is more money exchanged there daily than in the entire state of Utah. It is a police precinct by itself. The mall is an X-shaped shopping plan on three levels, containing over two hundred stores. Some walkways are marble; some are carpeted. In some areas, the "room-tone" is intimate, hushed; in others, sounds are magnified as in an underground cave. The Muzak is the same everywhere, and the temperature is always 72°. Whether one sees it as a shoppers' paradise or a claustrophobic nightmare, there is no denying that Woodfield is a superb example of an homogenized environment, the shopping mall par excellence, and, perhaps, the new "downtown" of the automotive suburbs.

Although the shopping center is often located in close proximity to, or actually along a commercial strip, it is, in many ways, quite a different road artifact. While the center is usually accessible only by car, it is planned as an immense "walking city" complex, in a way reminiscent of the American walking city of the early nineteenth century. Sometimes the center is called a "mall" to denote its token devotion to the pedestrian. Other times, center promoters resort to historic themes; for example, Emilo Zappia's re-creation of Benjamin Franklin's Philadelphia in the Independence Mall outside of Wilmington (Delaware), or the White Flint Mall (Washington, D.C.), a deliberate re-creation of nineteenth-century urban street facsimiles, which aspire to give the shopper an experience of Victorian city life without the danger of it. Other "modern" American shopping centers come equipped with colonial-style fronts, gas street lamps, cigar store Indians, barber poles, and even actors hired to play street characters.

The strip and the center differ in still other ways. The strip can be characterized as more loose, open, and out-of-doors. Stores can be torn down and replaced; owners and the goods they offer may change overnight. The center is roofed-in, and the range of stores is not as open-ended, but designed as a "package" of stores tightly controlled to fit its owner's expectations of volume and profit.

Both the strip and center, however, like so much of commercial archaeology, are highly elaborate symbolic systems. Architect Robert Venturi recommends two ways to begin an analysis of such symbols. In his proposals for how we might "learn from Las Vegas," he alerts us to be watching for "ducks" and "decorated sheds" (Figs. 48 and 49) among the plethora of commercial material culture we drive by everyday. Wherever we encounter artifacts characterized by an overall symbolic form, we have a kind of building-becoming-

Fig. 46. Country Plaza shopping center in Kansas City, Missouri, 1926. *Country Plaza Corp.*

Fig. 47. Country Plaza shopping center in Kansas City, Missouri, fall of 1967. *Paul D. Steffee.*

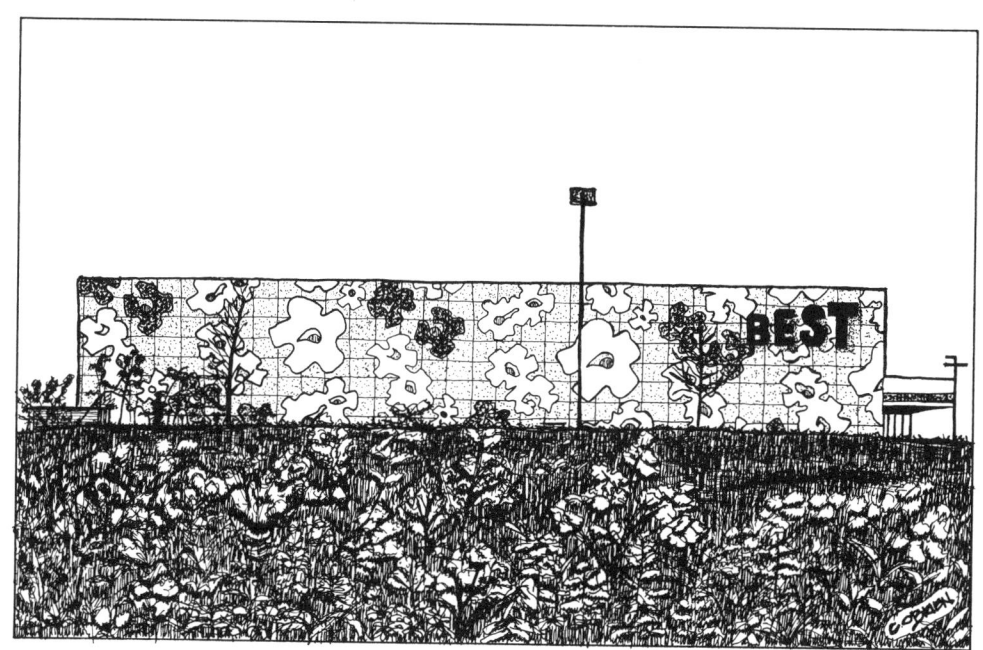

Fig. 48. An artist's impression of the "decorated shed," a major component, says architect Robert Venturi, of commercial art and strip architecture. *Cheryl O'Brien.*

Fig. 49. An artist's impression of what architect Robert Venturi refers to as "the duck," a kind of building-becoming-sculpture that frequently appears on the American roadscape. *Cheryl O'Brien.*

sculpture that Venturi calls "*the duck.*" This name he chose to honor the duck-shaped drive-in, "The Long Island Duckling," in Folksville, New York, that exemplifies the genre. Whenever we find structures with ornament applied independently to them, then Venturi says we are in the presence of "*the decorated shed.*" The duck is a special building that *is* a symbol; the decorated shed is the conventional shelter that *applies* symbols. Ducks, as we have already seen, are part of the post-World War I roadside. Decorated sheds form a major component of commercial art and strip architecture. It is therefore imperative, says Venturi, for the landscape historian to concern himself with the identification, classification, and interpretation of "the symbolism of the ugly and the ordinary in architecture and for the particular significance of the decorated shed with a rhetorical front and a conventional behind: for architecture as shelter with symbols on it."

Venturi and others have been iconologists worthy of our imitation, coining a riot of new nomenclature for the architectural imagery they have discovered along the supposedly "ugly and ordinary" contemporary landscape: Miami Moroccan; International Jet Set; Hollywood Orgasmic; Yamasaki Bernini; Nieymeyer Moorish; Gourmet Mansardic; Moorish Tudor Arabian Knights; Bauhaus Hawaiian. Although these typologies and stylistic categorizations are, in part, deliberate parodies of the inherent difficulties in applying traditional art history canons to many twentieth-century buildings, they also point up the need for an approach such as above-ground archaeology, so as to be able to look at the American landscape with a new perspective.

II A Road Guide to U.S. 40 in Indiana, Past and Present

A Note On Method

In attempting to decide on the most appropriate way to explore U.S. 40 as an above-ground archaeological site, I once considered, albeit in jest, the idea of having a 156-mile canopy constructed, much as the contemporary sculptor Javacheff Christo builds massive artworks on the landscape, along the length of the entire highway as it crossed central Indiana. At appropriate entrances and exits to the road, billboards would alert people to their everyday involvement in this open-air historical archive, library, and museum, where local and community history could be discovered and interpreted in a personal and novel way. With a field guide such as this book in hand, they might realize that there are many extraordinary but untold stories in the ordinary artifacts of the road that they encounter. In short, employing the general techniques of above-ground archaeology to read the history on the land might help us to recognize and interpret the past as it survives in the present, with a vividness and intimacy that would enable any of us to discover the delight of "doing history" on our own and on a locale that we as twentieth-century Americans know so well: the road and the roadscape.

While my fantasy of an intrastate historical exhibit remains a whim, the spirit of it motivates this essay. My hope is that readers will come to see U.S. 40 in Indiana as not only a case study of one way to do above-ground archaeology, but also as a way of experiencing an environment that is a living, changing landscape full of historical intrigue and contemporary insight. To know U.S. 40, and by inference any American roadscape, one must embark on an intellectual and geographical odyssey. That is to say, one must confront the roadscape directly, by walking or riding over it as well as by exploring it vicariously in reading what others have written, photographed, mapped, sung, or exhibited of it. One needs to do both reading and roaming on and about the road.

In exploring U.S. 40 in Indiana, I have roamed slightly beyond the state's borders to see what the route looked like east as far as Zanesville, Ohio, and west to Vandalia, Illinois. The reason for this was because this inclusive two-hundred-mile stretch was the third section of the original National Road to be designated and built in the early nineteenth century. Unlike the first two sections, one running from Cumberland, Maryland, to Wheeling, West Virginia, and a second from Wheeling to Zanesville, Ohio, this third segment is very representative of the midwestern heartland, traversing three states of the Old Northwest Territory and completely bisecting Indiana.

While I have focused my attention principally on the route that U.S. 40 follows through Indiana, I have also roamed off that road (and encourage others to do likewise) into the numerous towns and cities, counties, and townships through which the road travels. This

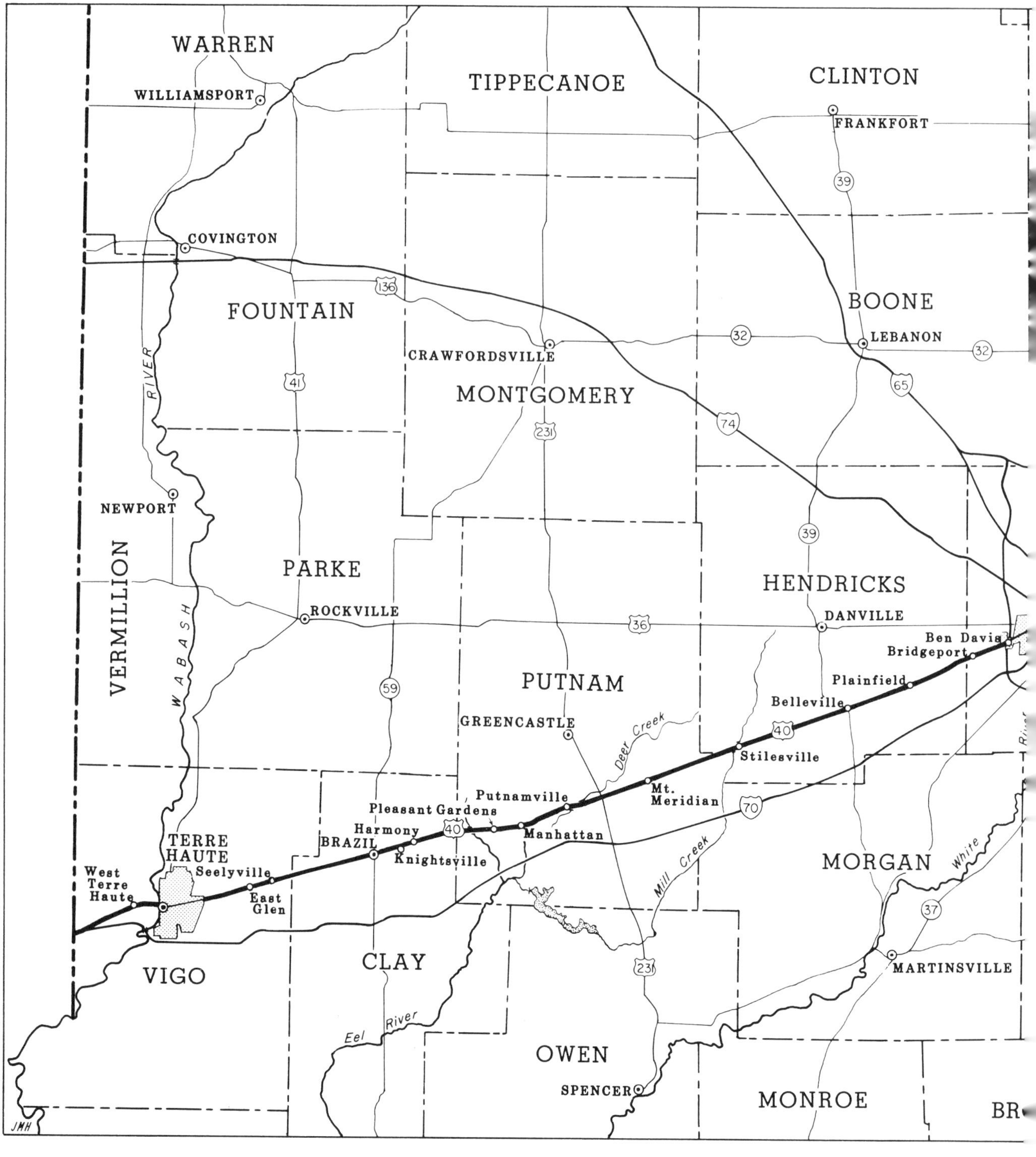

WARREN
WILLIAMSPORT
TIPPECANOE
CLINTON
FRANKFORT
39
COVINGTON
136
FOUNTAIN
BOONE
32
LEBANON
32
CRAWFORDSVILLE
41
RIVER
MONTGOMERY
65
231
74
NEWPORT
VERMILLION
WABASH
PARKE
39
HENDRICKS
ROCKVILLE
36
DANVILLE
Ben Davis
Bridgeport
Plainfield
PUTNAM
59
Belleville
GREENCASTLE
Deer Creek
40
Stilesville
Mt. Meridian
Putnamville
Pleasant Gardens
70
Harmony
40
Manhattan
BRAZIL
TERRE HAUTE
Knightsville
MORGAN
White
West Terre Haute
Seelyville
East Glen
Mill Creek
37
VIGO
CLAY
231
MARTINSVILLE
Eel River
OWEN
SPENCER
MONROE
JMH

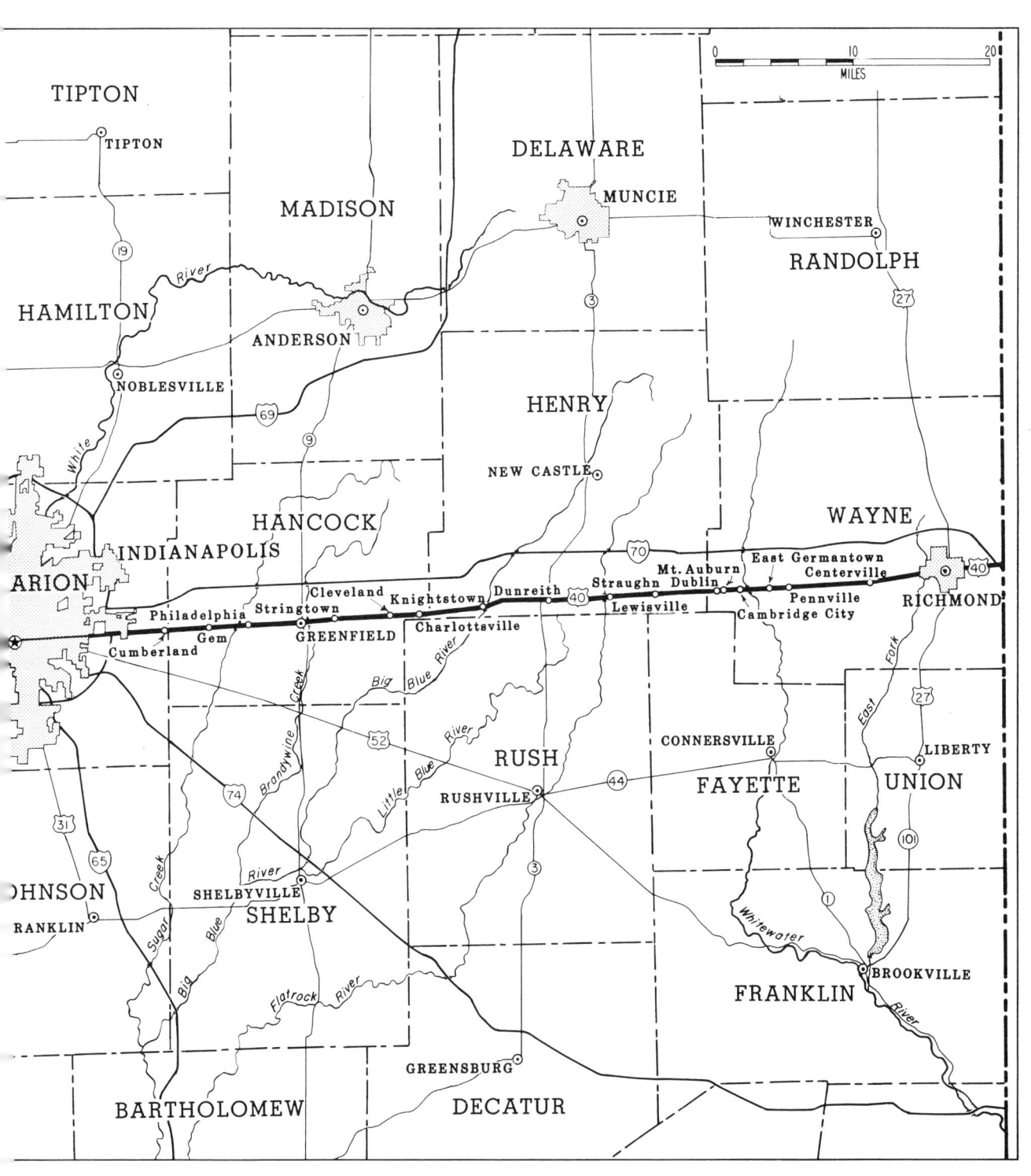

John Hollingsworth, Bloomington

has meant that I have permitted my above-ground archaeological site to include not only U.S. 40 and its proximate roadside, but also an eight-county corridor of landscape—Wayne, Henry, Hancock, Marion, Hendricks, Putnam, Clay, and Vigo counties, traveling east to west—in which the road has been an integral historical and cultural feature for over one hundred and fifty years.

Despite these attempts to define my research, I recognize that this road guide is impressionistic rather than a systematic study. Above-ground archaeology has no pretensions to being an exact science; it is, at its core, an art—especially an art of looking at the interactions of the past in the present and the present in the past. Hence, in providing the guidelines that follow, the aim has been to be enlightening rather than encyclopedic, engaging rather than exhaustive.

In developing this perspective on U.S. 40 I have, understandably, learned from the perspectives of many others who also look closely at the road and roadscape. For instance, throughout this volume are included examples of the ways that other students of the road, past and present, have envisioned and communicated their sense of its meaning. These include the perspectives of the cartographer, the landscape architect, the highway designer, the tourism department director, the marketing analyst, the artist, the highway patrol officer, the novelist, the urban planner, the highway maintenance engineer, and, of course, the documentary photographer.

All of these methods for comprehending the roadscape have been used in this application of above-ground archaeology and its cross-disciplinary approach. Since the approach is a process, a way of learning by doing, I have tried to emphasize the methods of reading the extant physical environment of U.S. 40 across time during the various historical periods of its existence and across space in the several aspects of everyday life. I propose, therefore, that we examine U.S. 40, first, as to its historical development and, second, as to its contemporary meaning.

National Road: 1827-1849

What survives along present-day U.S. 40 to remind us of the route's earliest and most celebrated (at least in written histories) role as a part of the famous 677-mile National Road, the first major road to be built with federal funds in this country and the most important overland route linking the Midwest with the Atlantic seaboard in the early nineteenth century? What can we learn of the history of this national highway, proposed in 1784 by George Washington and Albert Gallatin, first financed by Congress in 1805 during Thomas Jefferson's administration, and surveyed and constructed across Indiana from Richmond to Terre Haute between 1827 and 1839?

Place-names are perhaps one of the most obvious types of evidence of this era of the road's history. Road signs tell us, for instance, of the location of the original "Old National Road" laid out in the 1830s, as well as one of its later realignments as the new "National Road." As U.S. 40 moves through several Indiana towns, it is often still locally called the National Road, National Pike, National Avenue, or Cumberland Street or Avenue. The latter place-name is derived from the official government name for the route, so designated because it began in Cumberland, Maryland. In turn, Cumberland, Indiana (platted in 1831), in Marion County, was so named because it grew up directly along the Cumberland Road. While Dublin in Wayne County was probably named for the Irish city, a local anecdote, related by Ronald L. Baker and Marvin Carmony in *Indiana Place Names* (1975), also attributes the town's origins to its role on the National Road: "Dublin, in the early days, was a famous mudhole just west of Cambridge City. Wagons and stagecoaches when passing this spot had to double team to get through. When the town was platted (1831), it was decided to call it Dublin, because of always having to double team at that place."

Knightstown, in Henry County, owes its name and location to its being platted in 1827 by Jonathan Knight, the federal commissioner in charge of surveying and overseeing of construction of the route across Indiana. To Knight, we are also indebted for his early above-ground archaeological assessments of the countryside through which the road passed: Knight's original survey field notes in four volumes (now in the National Archives) give a valuable description of the Indiana landscape in 1827, including the location of mileposts and the names of settlers and structures along the route; Knight also left a detailed twelve-foot topographical map of the road's course across the state as he projected it (Figs. 51 and 52).

Although we have no actual physical examples of the original dirt, gravel, and later macadamized road surface of the National Road in Indiana, we can gain a sense of its width and scale along an abandoned section of its route in Putnam County, or by driving the spur road from Raysville to Ogden in Henry County. When compared with early photography of the road and Knight's description of the construction methods first employed to build the road, we can recapture something of the historical ambience of early overland transport. Historical drawings and old photographs also help us reconstruct the now demolished road engineering achievements such as the famous first bridges across the White River at Indianapolis (see Fig. 13) and the Whitewater River at Richmond (Fig. 53). The zealous landscape historian also can still discover in the field the stone abutments of the 1833-36 Richmond bridge along the banks of the Whitewater.

Unfortunately the typical milestones once used to mark one's progress, at between six and twelve miles an hour, on a typical National Road journey are no longer astride the thoroughfare. Several original milestones, however, still survive along U.S. 40 in Ohio. The number at the top of each of these stones informed travelers how far they were from Cumberland, Maryland, where a marker stands today, denoting the spot in the corner of lot No. 1 where David Schriver, first superintendent of construction, began the road. In pointing his transit from this beginning milestone in Cumberland, Schriver was consciously replicating a road building tradition that started with the Romans, who marked all their major highways from the golden milestone that stood in the center of the Roman Forum. It was not without reason, therefore, that nineteenth-century American orators were wont to describe the National Road as their country's Appian Way. A milestone on the National Road between Richmond and Centerville is shown in Fig. 54.

Several early structures that once serviced that road are still evident along the U.S. 40 route in Indiana. Among the first business ventures to appear along the road were blacksmith and wagon shops, such as those that the above-ground archaeologist finds in Dublin and Centerville. These, together with a tavern (e.g., like the one formerly at Mount Meridian, now relocated as an antique shop in Greencastle) and a general store, marked the beginning of many a new town along the new road. East Germantown, founded in 1827, Belleville in 1829, Stilesville in 1828, and Manhattan in 1829 grew in exactly that way.

Also located along the road were wagon house yards and drovers' stands, where tired horses rested overnight beside their great loads, often packed into Conestoga wagons, named for the Conestoga River Valley of Pennsylvania where they were first made. At such sites, drovers corralled herds of hogs, cattle, sheep, even turkeys for the night. Just west of Cambridge City, Indiana, in Mount Auburn, still stands the Huddleston House (Fig. 55), built in the early 1840s, a handsome three-story, Federal-style brick home, where numerous emigrant wagons camped on their

Fig. 50. An artist's recording of East Washington Street, the route of the old National Road through Indianapolis, during the flood of 1847. Drawing by Christian Schrader. *Indiana State Library.*

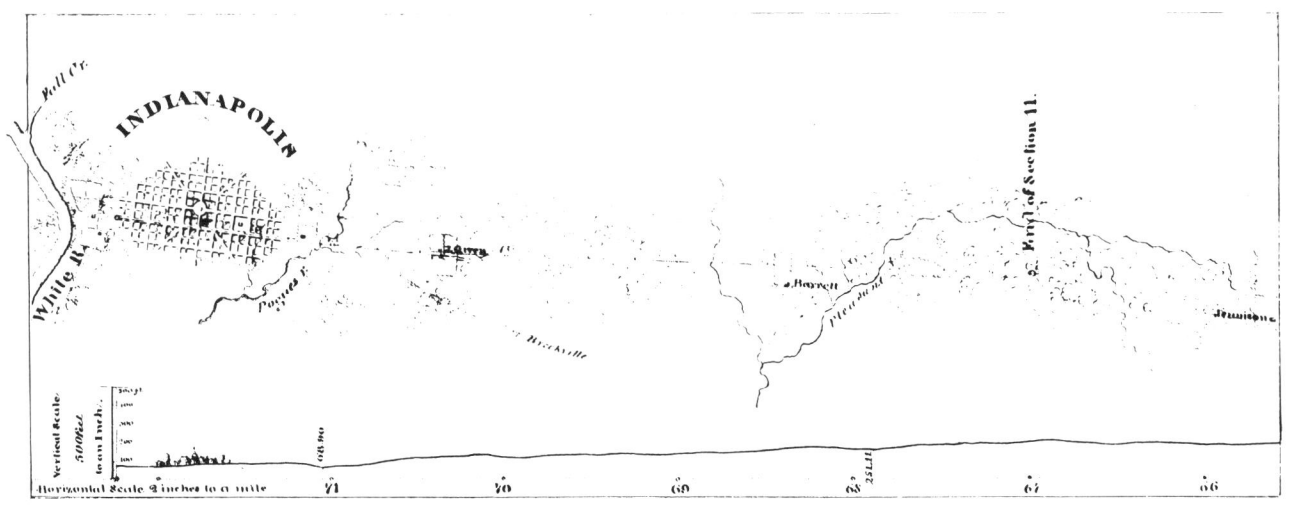

Fig. 51. Section of Jonathan Knight's field map of the Cumberland Road (the old National Road) as it passed through Indianapolis and the area to the east, 1827. *National Archives and Records Service.*

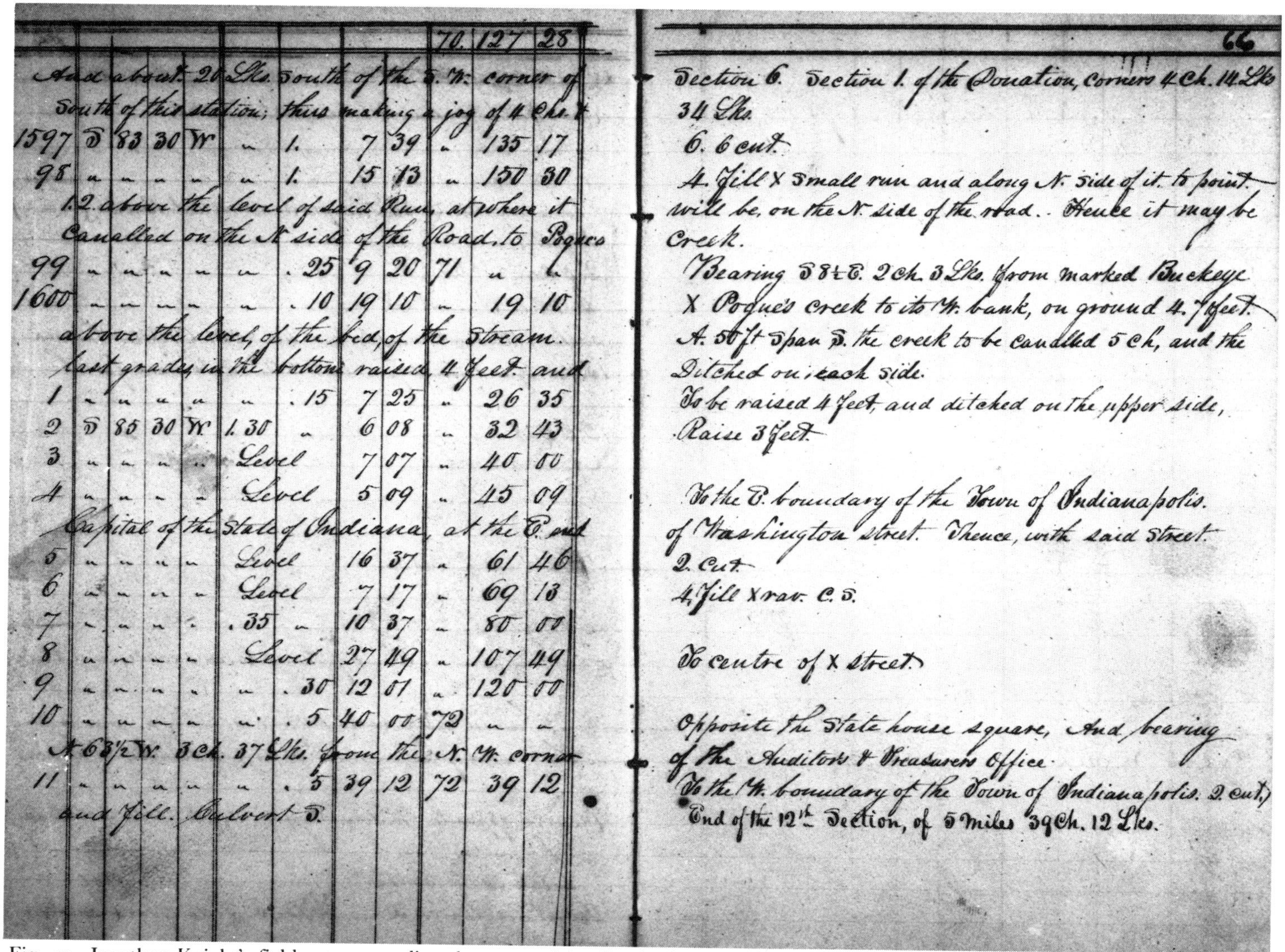

70 127 28

And about 20 Lks. South of the S. W. corner of South of this station; thus making a jog of 4 Chs. &

1597 S 83 30 W ~ 1. 7 39 ~ 135 17

98 ~ ~ ~ ~ ~ 1. 15 13 ~ 150 30

1.2. above the level of said Run, at where it Canalled on the N. side of the Road, to Pogues

99 ~ ~ ~ ~ ~ .25 9 20 71 ~ ~

1600 ~ ~ ~ ~ ~ .10 19 10 ~ 19 10

above the level of the bed of the Stream. last grades in the bottom raised 4 feet and

1 ~ ~ ~ ~ ~ .15 7 25 ~ 26 35

2 S 85 30 W 1.30 ~ 6 08 ~ 32 43

3 ~ ~ ~ ~ Level 7 07 ~ 40 00

4 ~ ~ ~ ~ Level 5 09 ~ 45 09

Capital of the State of Indiana, at the E. end

5 ~ ~ ~ ~ Level 16 37 ~ 61 46

6 ~ ~ ~ ~ Level 7 17 ~ 69 13

7 ~ ~ ~ ~ .35 ~ 10 37 ~ 80 00

8 ~ ~ ~ ~ Level 27 49 ~ 107 49

9 ~ ~ ~ ~ ~ .30 12 01 ~ 120 00

10 ~ ~ ~ ~ ~ .5 40 00 72 ~ ~

N. 63½ W. 3 Ch. 37 Lks. from the N. W. corner

11 ~ ~ ~ ~ ~ .5 39 12 72 39 12

and Fill. Culvert S.

66

Section 6. Section 1. of the Donation, corners 4 Ch. 14 Lks 34 Lks.

6. 6 cut.

4. Fill X Small run and along N. side of it to point will be, on the N. side of the road. Hence it may be Creek.

Bearing S 8½ E. 2 Ch. 3 Lks. from marked Buckeye

X Pogue's creek to its W. bank, on ground 4.7 feet.

A. 50 ft Span S. the creek to be canalled 5 Ch, and the Ditched on each side.

To be raised 4 feet, and ditched on the upper side,

Raise 3 feet.

To the E. boundary of the Town of Indianapolis. of Washington street. Thence, with said Street.

2. Cut.

4. Fill X rav. C. S.

To centre of X street.

Opposite the State house square, And bearing of the Auditors & Treasurers Office

To the W. boundary of the Town of Indianapolis. 2 cut,

End of the 12th Section, of 5 miles 39 Ch. 12 Lks.

Fig. 52. Jonathan Knight's field notes recording the route of the Cumberland Road (the old National Road) through Indianapolis, 1827. *National Archives and Records Service.*

Fig. 53. The National Road covered bridge over the Whitewater River in Richmond, Indiana, ca. 1890. *IHS.*

way west. Part of the wagon yard is still extant, as are the outdoor oven (where travelers were at liberty to do communal baking) and the summer kitchen (to which the "movers," as they were called, had access for twenty-five cents a night).

Local legend has long maintained that the Huddleston House was also a National Road tavern and inn, but current research by the Historic Landmarks Foundation of Indiana (which occupies the building as the organization's eastern regional office) suggests that the original owners never served public meals, hard liquor, or made a regular practice of renting sleeping rooms. To investigate a typical road tavern and inn of the mid-nineteenth century, the landscape historian should stop at the Vinton House (now the Schwegman Hotel) in Cambridge City, or the Old State Road Inn, one mile south of Lewisville.

Such indoor accommodations were usually provided by a tavern with sleeping facilities or an inn with ample capacity to "water the horses and brandy the gentlemen." In addition to servicing transients, such road shelters were community centers. Local residents visited their public rooms for news and gossip and crowded their halls during court sessions and for dances, theatrical performances, lodge meetings, and even church services.

Inns and taverns also spawned a type of road artifact, outdoor advertising, that has been part of the roadscape ever since. Artistic signboards, now avidly sought by museum curators and private collectors

Fig. 54. Milestone on the National Road between Richmond and Centerville, Indiana, ca. 1890, indicating the state line between Indiana and Ohio to be 9 miles distant, Richmond 4½ miles, and Centerville 1 mile. *Indiana State Library.*

alike, once beckoned travelers to stay at Bayles' Sign of the Green Tree in Richmond, the White Hall Tavern in Centerville, or the Eagle and Lion in Terre Haute. Many of the hosts used their own names, such as Dillon's in Knightstown, Hartsock's at Bridgeport, or Cunningham's west of Brazil. Others displayed their patriotism by calling their establishments Washington Hall or Union Hotel (Indianapolis), Eagle House (Putnamville), or the American House Inn (Centerville). A hundred-mile-or-so portrait gallery of sorts once lined the road with likenesses of Franklin, General Washington, Tecumseh, and Clay. Like the names of several of the counties (e.g., Wayne, Henry, Marion, Putnam, Hancock) through which U.S. 40 passes, early tavern names were a roll call of American Revolutionary and early national heroes of the republic.

In above-ground archaeological research, one occasionally comes upon a large site such as a long street, a whole neighborhood, even a complete town that might be called an *epitome district*. By means of its total environment—building types, architectural styles, public and private spaces, and land use—an epitome district encapsulates a past chronological era with a special poignancy and power through its distinctive concentration of artifacts of one time in one place. For example, is there not a heightened sense of the 1870s urban America in Indianapolis's Woodruff Place? of an 1840s waterfront community in the Riverside district in Evansville? of an early nineteenth-century planned communitarian experiment in New Harmony? or the antebellum Midwest in the Old Richmond Historic District?

Centerville, Indiana, immediately strikes the landscape historian as a community aptly representative of the National Road era of U.S. 40. Located at the center of Wayne County, it was the county seat from 1818 to 1873, when the seat of government was transferred to Richmond. Centerville was the only community besides Indianapolis in existence between Richmond and Terre Haute along the route that Jonathan Knight surveyed for the new federal thoroughfare in 1827. The boom days of National Road traffic accelerated the population increase and land use that had already begun in the decade after the community had been declared the county seat. Lots in Centerville sold rapidly and land values rose quickly. Some of the streets, originally 100 feet wide, were narrowed to 60

Fig. 55. The restored Huddleston House on U.S. 40 in Mount Auburn, Indiana, 1983. IHS—*Seldon Bradley.*

and even 40 feet, as people began attaching additions to structures originally set back from the road; new building construction was at times flush with the sidewalk. Maximum space utilization was evident in new houses built with common side walls, creating Centerville's Federal-style row housing. This building boom was also responsible for Centerville's archway architecture: the original houses, no longer on the main street, could only be reached by leaving passageways between the new facades. Even the space above these passageways was utilized for additional room.

Centerville, with its modest brick and frame dwellings, has almost all the material culture remains of a typical National Road town *in situ*: the Lantz wagon shop (212-214 West Main), the American House Inn (101 West Main), the Mansion House stagecoach station (214 East Main), the Old Cumberland Church (110-112 North Morton), a blacksmith shop, and several imposing town residences—such as the Rown House (210 East Main), the Rariden House (120 West Main), and the Greek Revival home (319 West Main) of Oliver P. Morton, Indiana's Civil War governor. All that is visually missing from this town-as-museum setting are the stone blocks (one to two feet in length, six inches broad, and a foot wide) that once constituted the paving of the National Road as it passed through the town. This was the first section of the route in Indiana to be so paved—the road blocks were quarried southeast of Centerville, finished as smooth as building stone, and laid with wonderful precision. Local historian Arthur Whallon, writing in *Centerville, Indiana: A National Road Town* (1970), speculates that "there are probably still enough of the old stones left beneath modern U.S. 40 to build a court house."

In the past decade, Centerville has capitalized on its historic architecture and become a major tourist attraction. Much of what we have called its *epitome district* has also been designated as a historic district by both state and federal historic preservation agencies. A sense of its own historicity has, in turn, engendered a new local industry, antique dealerships, that now confront the landscape observer at practically every storefront or through any alley passageway. If one wants to observe a busy landscape of memorabilia wheeling and dealing, Centerville is the place to go. Many consider it the "Antique Capital of Indiana." At any of its

Fig. 56. The old Wayne County Courthouse on the old National Road in Centerville, Indiana, ca. 1890. Centerville was the county seat from 1818 to 1873. *Historic Centerville, Inc.*

Fig. 57. Looking east on Main Street, the old National Road, from Main Cross in Centerville, Indiana, ca. 1900. *Historic Centerville, Inc.*

Fig. 58. A sample of the archway architecture on Main Street (U.S. 40) in Centerville, Indiana, 1983. *IHS—Seldon Bradley.*

numerous retail shops, flea markets, auctions, or special antique festivals, one might come upon such momentoes as a stagecoach driver's bugle, an emigrant's guidebook, or a postal rate broadside of the National Road era that helped put Centerville on the road map in the first place.

Historical consciousness of the impact of the National Road is also discernable along the U.S. 40 route where there have been deliberate attempts to create historic markers and monuments. With the notable exception of the stone marker in Plainfield, designating the site where President Martin Van Buren (an opponent of internal improvements supported by the federal treasury) was "accidently" dumped from his stagecoach into the mud in 1842 as an object lesson of the importance of keeping the highway in good repair, historical markers on the road are almost all east of Indianapolis. Historical markers concerned with the National Road can be found in front of the Indiana State Capitol (see Figs. 59 and 60), at the intersection of U.S. 40 and Interstate 465, as well as at the Knights-town Spring (Fig. 131). The American Liberty Commission has also put up a highway historic marker, in imitation of the typical Indiana state highway marker, in commemoration of the National Road just west of Knightstown. The Madonna of the Trail monument (Fig. 61) in Richmond's Glen Miller Park culminates or initiates (depending on whether you are traveling east or west) this string of deliberate historical memorials in Indiana. The Madonna, one of twelve such sculptures placed on the National Old Trails Road from Maryland to California by the DAR, was unveiled in 1928. The increasing density of National Road markers continues as such monuments become even more frequent the farther east one travels.

Historical sites and markers can also be considered above-ground archaeological evidence. They always contain at least two significant messages. In addition to conveying factual historical information about the specific, person, or place that they are designed to commemorate, historical markers also tell us a great deal about what was important to the generation that

Fig. 59. National Road monument at the south entrance to the Indiana State Capitol on West Washington Street (U.S. 40) in Indianapolis, 1984. *IHS—Seth Rossman.*

Fig. 60. National Road monument put up by the American Society of Civil Engineers in 1976 at the southwest corner of the Indiana State Capitol grounds on Washington Street (U.S. 40) in Indianapolis, 1984. *IHS—Seth Rossman.*

first set them in place and to the people who continue to preserve and maintain them as civic totems. In pursuing such an inquiry with the assortment of historical markers and monuments that we encounter along U.S. 40, we should note carefully several facts: a) where the historic markers are actually placed on the landscape; b) when they were put in place; c) who in the community designated and funded the landmarks; and, d) which historical events or personalities are consistently noticed or neglected in an area's past.

Private Highway Associations: 1850-1925

If we were to apply the simple formula described above to the history of U.S. 40 in the second half of the nineteenth century, we would be left with the startling realization that, if the historical markers are to be believed, nothing of any consequence happened once the National Road was turned over to the state in 1849. No historical markers tell us anything of the seventy-five-year period when the road was influenced more by private associations than public agencies.

Even other above-ground archaeological evidence for this era of U.S. 40 history is scant. Unlike the artifacts of the route's genesis as the National Road, much of its late nineteenth-century history has been obliterated by successive road redevelopment throughout the twentieth century. Yet, some of its physical features do remain, and they are clues to what might be called an era of private control and public neglect of the road.

Two nineteenth-century technological innovations, the railroad and the automobile, initially influenced this private control of the road, a development which, in turn, produced two types of roads along the U.S. 40 route: the toll roads such as that run by the Central Plank Road Company in the 1850s and the private highway maintained by independent organizations like the National Old Trails Association in the 1910s. The first was primarily local in its scope, while the second attempted to create a national network of overland transport.

The railroad's impact on nineteenth-century surface travel is still evident by the abundant trackage that remains along both sides of U.S. 40 and crisscrosses the route innumerable times. In 1851, two years after the federal government had turned over the National Road to the state, the Terre Haute and Indianapolis Railroad Company was organized by Chauncey Rose and began construction as the second railroad to be completed in Indiana. A year later the first train was run over the completed line, and the following year the Indiana Central Railroad, connecting Indianapolis and Richmond, was in operation. Suddenly the National Road, originally touted as the most advanced

Fig. 61. Madonna of the Trail monument in Glen Miller Park, on U.S. 40 in Richmond, Indiana, erected in 1928 by the DAR, 1984. *IHS—Seth Rossman.*

form of overland travel yet devised by man, was paralleled for its entire distance across the state by a new type of road—the iron road—now proclaimed as the transport miracle of the nineteenth century.

The state of Indiana, which earlier had been engaged in a financially disastrous scheme of internal improvements involving canal building, wanted as little involvement as possible in highway construction and maintenance, particularly if railroads were to be the transportation networks of the future. Consequently, control of the National Road through Hancock, Marion, Hendricks, and Putnam counties was granted in 1849 to the Central Plank Road Company, which proceeded to cover the road with oak planks and put up a series of tollgates and tollhouses. In Indianapolis, a tollgate was built at the White River bridge and another just east of town (Fig. 62). An English traveler, J. Richard Beste who visited Indiana in 1851, noted in his book, *The Wabash* (1855), that tolls were not required to be paid on the Central Plank Road by those "going to or returning from Militia musterings, from any religious meeting on the Sabbath, or from any state, town, or county election, or from any funeral procession."

Through Wayne County the road was taken over by the Wayne County Turnpike Company which operated it as a toll road for the next forty years, until it was finally purchased by the townships through which it passed and made a free gravel road by 1893. In Henry County the road was also controlled by a private company. These early toll roads, unlike the present-day Northern Indiana Toll Road, left few traces on our contemporary landscape. We know of

Fig. 62. Abandoned tollhouse on East Washington Street (U.S. 40) in Indianapolis, near its present intersection with Shadeland Avenue, ca. 1890. *Indiana State Library*.

Fig. 63. A section west of Brazil, Indiana, of the right-of-way of the abandoned interurban line that ran along U.S. 40 from Indianapolis to Terre Haute, 1983. *IHS—Seldon Bradley.*

them largely through county histories and atlases, travelers' accounts, some surviving photography, and an occasional place-name.

Local toll roads offered little competition to the interstate railroads or their progeny, the interurban lines that also paralleled the U.S. 40 by the turn of the century. In fact, the careful observer can still spot two relict interurban line bridges and an abandoned stretch of right-of-way for the transit company that once connected Terre Haute and Indianapolis (Fig. 63). Spring Lake, a small community along U.S. 40 just west of Greenfield, owes its existence primarily to an interurban line. William Dye created a spring-fed artificial lake on this Hancock County site in 1884-85 and also laid out a picnic grounds that was originally called Dye's Grove. An interurban spur was later connected with the resort, and the area became a trolley park known as Spring Lake when it was platted in 1912 (Figs. 64 and 65). Unfortunately, most of the depots or car barns of traction lines, like the one to Spring Lake and like many stations and terminals of the larger railroad companies, have met the wrecker's ball.

Recreational activities, particularly bicycling and early auto touring, were largely responsible for the revival of the U.S. 40 route as a transportation corridor at the turn of the twentieth century. Although these mechanical contraptions often frightened horses and occasionally threatened the lives and limbs of their users, participants in the bicycle craze, equipped with maps (Fig. 67) and moxie, rode out of cities such as Indianapolis and along the old National Road, intent on making "century rides" of a hundred miles or more.

As members of local chapters of the League of American Wheelmen, the cyclists fought for the right to ride on public thoroughfares and against the requirement that they dismount when meeting horses. Their persistent and organized efforts inspired a state and national crusade for better roads.

In this effort, the bicyclists were joined by the automobilists who, by the early 1900s, were clattering, vibrating, and rumbling along in their four-wheeled horseless carriages over city streets and the rutted National Road. Neglect of the road had permitted farmers to encroach on the right-of-way: fences, chicken coops, and barns had been built onto the original eighty-foot width. The real problem, however, was

Fig. 64. Interurban stop on the old National Road just west of Greenfield, Indiana, from which, in the summer, a special run was made to Spring Lake Park, ca. 1912. *IHS*.

Fig. 65. The "dinky" that made the run from the interurban stop (Fig. 64) on U.S. 40 to Spring Lake, passing under the Pennsylvania Railroad bridge over Sugar Creek, ca. 1912. *IHS*.

the roadbed—or lack of it. The macadam surface of the road's wagon-and-coach days was no longer satisfactory, since the faster autos fanned the dust binder from the crushed stone surfaces and blew it away. Drivers of the new "self-propelled machines," built in Indiana by firms such as Haynes, Auburn, Studebaker, and Maxwell, understandably joined the clamor for paved and wider roads. Early experiments in twentieth-century road surfacing with brick, asphalt, Portland cement, and eventually concrete are now only visible through the techniques of below-ground archaeology or by inspecting highway department work sites when the highway is under repair. One can also get a feel for the scale of the first paved sections along U.S. 40 in Indiana by driving the single lane of the old National Road in Wayne County or the abandoned leg of the Reelsville road in Putnam County.

Pioneer motorists using the National Road in 1900 were an adventuresome lot. Protecting their eyes from dust by means of goggles and wearing linen dusters to preserve their clothes, they ventured across the countryside. Their earliest overnight accommodations were "motor gypsy" camps set up by the side of the road for the night. Later they patronized municipal and private auto camps established in the 1920s outside of towns such as Belleville and Brazil.

Another prominent artifact of this road era was the private tourist home, where families rented out a few extra bedrooms for one dollar a night per room. Most rooms had free linen and a hot shower down the hall. Often run by couples such as Mr. and Mrs. Henry Eden in Plainfield, the homey decor and easy informality attracted families and traveling salesmen.

The occasional cluster of tourist cabins (Fig. 71) that the above-ground archaeologist finds along U.S. 40 outside Richmond (now converted to antique shops) and Terre Haute are other institutions of early auto touring. Individual cabins were usually arranged in either a straight line along the roadside or in a

A ROAD GUIDE TO U.S. 40   79

Fig. 66. Traction Terminal Station in Indianapolis, ca. 1910. It was demolished in 1972. *Indiana State Library*.

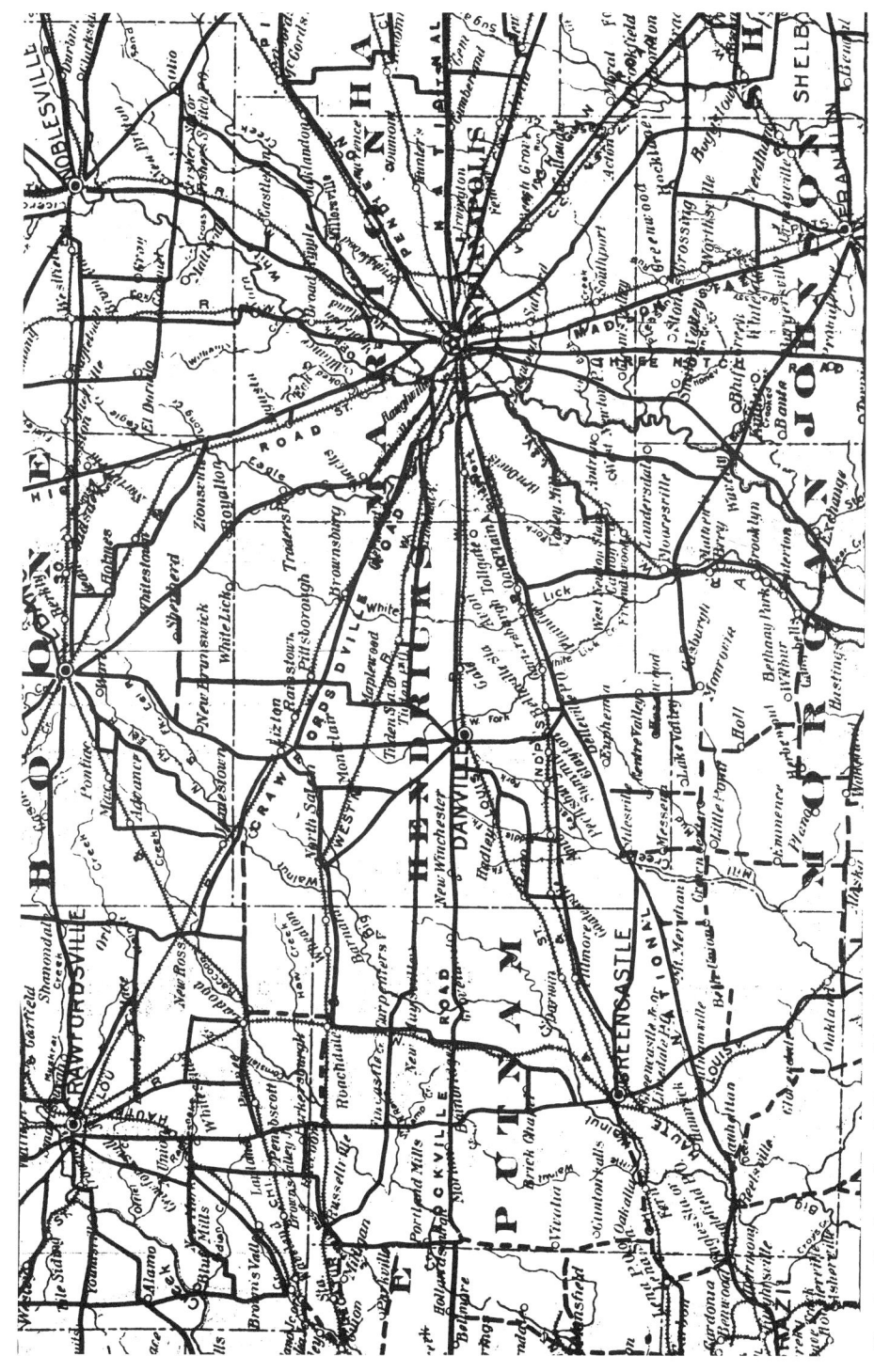

Fig. 67. Section of an Indiana bicycle road map, including the National Road through Putnam, Hendricks, and Marion counties, published by the Indiana Division League of American Wheelmen in 1896. *IHS.*

Fig. 68. Bicyclists posing by a house on the National Road in Greenfield, Indiana, ca. 1900. *IHS*.

U-shaped court around a gasoline station, store, and office. (See above, Figs. 43 and 44). In their heyday, the clean white paint, green shutters, small front porches with rockers, and window boxes with flowers all suggested the image of a home-away-from-home in which to spend a night off the road. In naming their cabins, entrepreneurs were ardent simplified spellers, a characteristic of much roadside signage ever since, preferring folksy phonetics to standard English. "U-Smile Kamp," "Kamp Kozy Kabins," and "U Wanna Kum Back" were particular favorites. Roadside wits also loved to call their humble establishments: "U Kum Inn," "Dew Drop Inn," or "U-Pop Inn." Today these tourist cabin ensembles are rapidly disappearing from the landscape or being converted into garages, chicken coops, or general storage facilities.

Tourist homes and tourist cabins served motorists who traveled U.S. 40 when it was known as the National Old Trails Road. Organized and promoted by executives in automotive and allied industries, as well as various local businessmen interested in encouraging interstate travel through their towns and cities, the National Old Trails Road was an attempt to develop a paved, all-weather, no-toll route from coast to coast by preserving and improving the old Cumberland Road east of the Mississippi and linking it with the Sante Fe Trail in the west. The dream of the National Old Trails Association was to make the old National Road (with a few exceptions, such as a detour through Dayton, Ohio) into a route that would extend 3,096 miles from Washington, D.C., to Los Angeles, California. As early as 1907 the Missouri Old Trails Road Association had proposed such a transcontinental highway, and at Kansas City in 1913, under the inspiration of Judge J. M. Lowe, a national organization was founded for the purposes of mapping and developing the overland route across the United States. The organization's principal objective was to convince local and state officials along that route to improve it, and local auto clubs to mark it with appropriate signage.

Modeled after the Lincoln Highway Association and the Dixie Highway Association, both largely the brainchild of Carl G. Fisher (Fig. 2), owner of Prest-O-Lite, an auto lamp company in Speedway, and founder of the Indianapolis Motor Speedway, the National Old Trails Association enlisted the help of auto clubs in cities such as Richmond, Indianapolis, and Terre Haute to sell memberships in the national association and to mark the auto trail in their communities by painting colored bands of red, white, and blue on fences, telephone and utility poles, and building corners at intersections along the route.

These early highway blazes and signs survive now only in museum collections and historical photography. They once brightened the Indiana roadside in a riot of colorful insignias. As a 1922 Rand McNally road map of Indiana shows, in addition to the National Old Trail and the Lincoln and Dixie highways, there were a Chicago Trail, a Range Line, a Belt Route, a Wabash Way, a Dunes Highway, and some twenty other roads marked by private highway associations and local touring clubs. The objective of all this trail marking, in addition to recalling earlier historic routes, was to provide twentieth-century motorists with what the National Road and other cross-country wagon trails had once furnished the first interstate immigrants—the assurance that if the traveler followed the trail, he would eventually arrive at his destination and not become lost.

The promoters of the National Old Trails Road, however, promised even more in their attempt to compete for traffic with the other major east-west transcontinental arteries like the Lincoln, Pike's Peak, or Ocean-to-Ocean highways. If one took the National Old Trails Road across the 13 states and 90 counties, and through 486 cities, towns, and villages, the association assured you that you were following the true course of American manifest destiny. This was so because the route followed the "isothermal line" that William Gilpin, in *Mission of the Northern American People, Geographical, Social, and Political* (1873), had proposed as the most influential geographical axis of both American and world civilization. "Along this axis," the promoters of the National Old Trails Road claimed in a large transcontinental map which they distributed, were "the great centers of population, the great cities of China, of India, Babylon, Jerusalem, Athens, Rome, Paris, London, Boston, New York, Philadelphia, Baltimore, Washington, Pittsburgh, Cincinnati, Columbus, Indianapolis, St. Louis, Kansas City, Topeka, Denver, Salt Lake City and San Francisco." Moreover, if one traveled the route of the red-white-and-blue blazes, the early twentieth-century American motorist was assured by the National Old Trails Road map that he was associating with a people who, in the past and in the present, possessed an "intense and intelligent energy" and from whom had come "our religion, our sciences, our civilization, our social manners, our arts, our agriculture, our domestic animals, and articles of food and raiment. . . ."

The touring potential of the National Old Trails Road was also promoted via broadsides, advertisements in volumes such as the American Automobile Association's yearly *Blue Book*, and on roadside billboards. The abandoned Old National Trail Restaurant (Fig. 72) at the intersection of routes 40 and 231 in Putnam County and the Old Trails Building on West Washington Street in Indianapolis (Fig. 73) are other reminders of the association's role in U.S. 40 history. The Old Trails Building, formerly the headquarters of the Old Trails Auto Insurance Company as well as for many years a state auto license bureau, is suitably bedecked with a romantic iconography of Indian heads and wagon trains that inspired early transcontinental auto touring along the U.S. 40 route.

If one were to select an Indiana town along the road that might serve as an epitome district of this road era from 1900 until the mid-1920s, Greenfield could be such a representative community. Although most famous as the birthplace of James Whitcomb Riley, who wrote poetry about the road that passed by his U.S. 40 homestead, the town, especially when studied in

Fig. 69. A Hoosier Motor Club touring group posing in front of the Prest-O-Lite factory in Speedway, Indiana,

before leaving on the Sociability Forty-Four Mile Run on May 16, 1920. *Bretzman Collection, IHS.*

Fig. 70. A stuck car being towed on an unidentified road in Indiana, ca. 1930. *Indiana State Highway Commission.*

conjunction with William Mitchell's stunning amateur photography of the community in the early twentieth century, enables one to appreciate what must have been the ambience of a typical Indiana highway town circa 1910. (The Mitchell photographs are in the Indiana Historical Society Library.) Still extant, for example, is much of the commercial architecture of Main Street, including such structures as the Romanesque Masonic Lodge (Fig. 74) that initially served as the town's community center only to be replaced in 1912 by the new Renaissance Revival commercial block up the street. (See Fig. 75.) Time collages abound on this segment of U.S. 40, particularly the marvelous contrast evident in the banking facades of an 1872 establishment and its modern counterpart across the street. The width and scale of the streetscape have not changed since William Mitchell captured the view from the famous Columbia Hotel (Fig. 76) at 118 East Main Street—the best place, in the estimate of the *Scarborough Official 1916 Tour Guide*, for the motorist to eat and spend the night while in the city. While no filling stations quite like the one Mitchell photographed survive (Fig. 78), there are still extant striking examples of service station architecture from the 1920s, as well as an impressive inventory of housing stock whose wide verandas embrace the U.S. 40 roadscape (Fig. 79). The turn-of-the-century homes recall an age when people lived out in public on their front porches, more intrigued by the passing parade of pedestrian and vehicular traffic and less absorbed in the private activities of their backyards or with their television sets indoors.

U.S. 40 Era: 1925-1960

Greenfield also contains some artifactual evidence of the advent of the "New Road" landscape that began to evolve after the federal numbered highway system came into existence in 1925. By that date the private road trails movement had got rather out of hand. There were at least two hundred and fifty marked trails sponsored by a hundred or more separate organizations, each with a headquarters and each collecting funds, issuing maps, promotional material, and road signs of every shape and size. Seventy percent of one trail coincided with other marked routes, and one trail overlapped as many as eleven others. One road carried eight different trail markers for a considerable distance. Many trails had alternate sections which further compounded the confusion, and one had alternates following three separate roads, all with the same name. The pressure of the trail associations for the improvement of their private trails made sensible and

Fig. 71. A cluster of one-time tourist cabins along U.S. 40 outside Richmond, Indiana, 1983. *IHS—Seldon Bradley.*

Fig. 72. The abandoned Old National Trail Restaurant, once a furniture store, at the intersection of U.S. 40 and Indiana 231 in Putnam County. *IHS—Seldon Bradley.*

Fig. 73. Old Trails Building and Entrance, 309 West Washington Street (U.S. 40) in Indianapolis, 1984. *IHS—Seth Rossman and Seldon Bradley, respectively.*

88   U.S. 40: A ROADSCAPE OF THE AMERICAN EXPERIENCE

Fig. 74. Masonic Lodge on the old National Road in Greenfield, Indiana, ca. 1910. *IHS*.

Fig. 75. The New Building on Main Street (the old National Road) in Greenfield, Indiana, ca. 1912. *IHS*.

A ROAD GUIDE TO U.S. 40

Fig. 76. The Columbia Hotel on Main Street (the old National Road) in Greenfield, Indiana, ca. 1900. *IHS.*

coordinated programming by state highway departments almost impossible.

The situation became so confused that in 1924-25 the American Association of State Highway Officials approved a resolution calling on the Secretary of Agriculture to name a board comprised of representatives from the Bureau of Public Roads and the state highway engineers to formulate a numbering and marking system of an interstate character for the principal highways of the United States. After two years of deliberation, a national numbered highway system of 96,626 miles was approved by the states to go into immediate effect all over the country. Twelve United States roads were originally designated in Indiana: three (U.S. 31, 41, 27) running north and south, and nine (U.S. 20, 24, 30, 36, 40, 50, 52, 110, 150) running east and west. Four of the U.S. highways passed through Indianapolis, by the early twentieth century a city which was already acting as the transportation hub of the state, and its principal route was U.S. 40. "When the system is inaugurated," the *Hoosier Motorist* proudly assured its readers in 1925, travelers "may head East on U.S. 40 and follow it to Baltimore, or he may head West and follow it to San Francisco, and his danger and direction markers will be uniform all the way."

To be sure, the familiar black-and-white shield

Fig. 77. Crowds gathered on Main Street (the old National Road) in Greenfield, Indiana, awaiting the arrival of the Hagenback & Wallace Circus, August 26, 1910. *IHS*.

markers are the most ubiquitous artifacts of U.S. 40's third life as a historical roadscape. While original, freestanding sculptured shields are not as widespread as those now painted on rectangular signs, both symbolize a truly momentous change in the American highway and its enormously expanded role in the American experience. Moreover, the shield, whose inspiration came from the United States seal which, in turn, owes its design to the iconography of Roman antiquity, has spawned other similar road signs: the emblems of Phillips 66 gasoline (which also takes part of its name from U.S. 66), the National American Ice Company, and even, in a muted form, the shield of the U.S. Interstate Highway System.

The advent of the federal highway numbering system coincided with what many above-ground archaeologists consider the heyday of the American road, a time when the road was widened and paved, when new architecture and building types appeared, and when automobile travel was elevated to a true adventure. John Margolies, writing in his survey *The End of the Road: Vanishing Highway Architecture* (1978), claims it was in the 1920s that this "Golden Age" began, lasting at least until World War II introduced gasoline rationing. The era witnessed the democratization of both the automobile and the roadside. Thanks to

Fig. 78. A 1920s filling station near Greenfield, Indiana. *IHS*.

Fig. 79. John Mitchell, Jr., editor of the *Hancock County Democrat*, poses with family and friends on the front porch of his home on the old National Road in Greenfield, Indiana, ca. 1910. *IHS*.

Henry Ford and other automakers, every American aspired to have his own car and get on the road; thanks to an expanding economy, many thought prosperity could be found in opening up a diner or a gas station, a motel or a truck stop along the road.

The physical road that we drive along today is largely a legacy of this exuberant U.S. 40 era. Starting in 1919, for example, the Indiana State Highway Department embarked on a quarter century of road expansion that accounts for the size and shape of the majority of roads we still use some six decades later. U.S. 40, as part of this program, was widened and resurfaced (Fig. 80). Expanding the road from three lanes to four lanes (initiated in the late 1920s) and dividing the highway (done on U.S. 40 throughout the late 1930s and the 1940s) also meant realigning and redirecting the route in several places. The above-ground archaeologist discovers much evidence of the latter phenomenon, particularly in the western counties where streams were approached and bridged differently, where more arduous terrain was traversed with easier gradients, and where whole towns, such as Reelsville and Pleasant Gardens, were bypassed because of the desire to create a "super highway" of better design and higher speed.

George R. Stewart, in his 1953 paean to *U.S. 40* as the greatest road in contemporary America, recognized and lauded this civil engineering achievement in his claim that U.S. 40 approached "close to perfection across the whole breadth of Indiana" and was "a finer highway over a longer distance in that state than in any other." Stewart was particularly impressed with what he called the archetype of the "highly developed modern highway," a portion of Indiana 40 constructed a mile and a half west of the Ohio-Indiana border on the eastern edge of Richmond. (See Figs. 83 and 84.) Here was the epitome of road design at mid-century: deep ravines filled in, hills bulldozed level, a concrete highway comprised of two twelve-foot eastbound lanes, two westbound lanes of equal breadth, and a forty-eight-foot separation strip. At the edges of the outside lanes were ten-foot gently sloping shoulders, and four-foot drainage ditches beyond which landscaped backslopes rose at a moderate grade to white posts marking the edge of the right-of-way. Also prominent in the design were at-grade crossovers for local traffic and various lanes permitting trucks to leave the highway, to stop at the weigh station, and to continue onward. Constructed in 1947, this road section was considered by the State Highway Commission to be the apex of road engineering. If it were to be constructed again, one official told Stewart, "there are no improvements that would be made over the present design." It survives, with Interstate 70 roaring over it, as a striking outdoor exhibit of the U.S. 40 era.

Also extant along U.S. 40 in Indiana are other little-noticed examples of the massive earth-moving and bridge-building of this period in the road's history. Major road relocations affording motorists better sight distance, wider radii of road curvature, and uniform grades can still be seen at Reelsville, Manhattan, and elsewhere in Putnam County. New reinforced concrete bridges replaced older metal bridges of both truss and trestle design. After the 1920s, concrete bridges became a common fixture on U.S. 40, easily identifiable as to date and type by consulting the American Association of State Highway Officials guide to *Standard Specifications for Highway Bridges* (1931), which served as the state's reference for bridge construction prior to World War II.

These new concrete bridges tended to be stark and streamlined, paralleling to a certain extent the Art Moderne architectural style of 1930 to 1945. That style is also evident along the road in structures like Danners, a general store in Knightstown (Fig. 85). The soft or rounded corners, flat roofs, and smooth-wall finishes created a distinctive streamlined or wind-tunnel look which characterizes the Art Moderne style, a style many interpreters see as appropriate to the Americans' increasing fascination with speed and

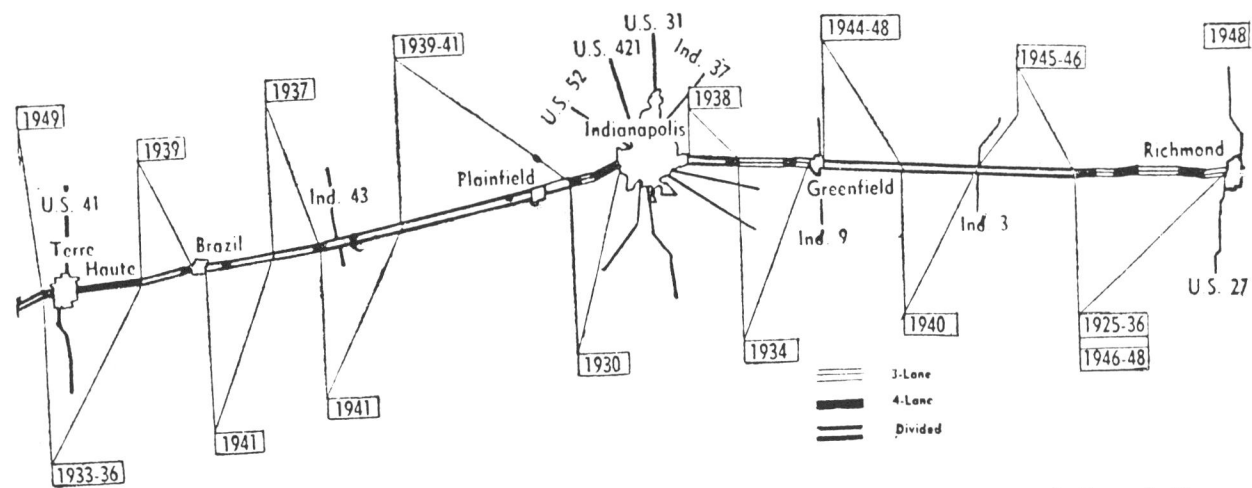

Fig. 80. Map showing the progress made in twenty years toward widening of U.S. 40 across Indiana. *Indianapolis News.*

Fig. 81. Dual laning of U.S. 40 west of Terre Haute, ca. 1940. *Martin Collection, IHS.*

94   U.S. 40: A ROADSCAPE OF THE AMERICAN EXPERIENCE

Fig. 82. U.S. 40 east of Putnamville, Indiana, with improved twenty-foot lanes and parkway, 1940. *National Archives and Records Service.*

efficiency. Evident in early Greyhound bus design, in automobiles (Fig. 86), and in roadside diners, the style made the first extensive use of aluminum and stainless steel as construction materials.

Road diners, such as those still in operation in Plainfield (Fig. 87) or in West Terre Haute, are one type of eatery that are reminiscent of U.S. 40's acme as a touring highway. Roadhouses, such as the now derelict Wander Inn at Reelsville, are a second type, and pop-art restaurants, like the Coffee Pot near Cambridge City (see Fig. 39), are a third. However, most of the whimsical short-order places that once presented themselves in buildings shaped like their products—chuck wagons, root beer barrels, or ice-cream cones—have been driven out of business by standardized national fast-food chains that now overpopulate the road.

Signs abound on U.S. 40. Some are particularly distinctive of the era between the wars. Unfortunately, only in museum exhibits and photographs do we still find the famous Burma-Shave sign sequences (Fig. 88), but the road is still littered with neon, an advertising innovation of the period that gave the highway a totally new ambience at night. Blinking, flashing, pulsating signs of every hue still beckon the U.S. 40 motorists to eat, drink, sleep, or play as they did in the 1930s. Assuredly a form of twentieth-century vernacular and commercial art, the neon sign tells us of other new artifacts that likewise appeared in the U.S. 40 era: drive-in movies, such as Cinema 40 and the National Drive-In; trailer parks and mobile home courts; the nationally designed, corporate gasoline station; and the early motel.

Motels, without a doubt, owe their origins and evolution to the American traveler's use, in increasing numbers, of the automobile. Unpretentious in its early form, the motel grew from obscurity out of other vernacular features of the American roadside, especially the auto camp and tourist home. Driving along U.S. 40, one can see this history unfold in a changing building morphology that suggests how this road artifact, originally designed as an alternative to hotel accommodations, has, in our own time, actually become quite hotel-like.

Fig. 83. U.S. 40 on the eastern outskirts of Richmond, Indiana, as photographed by George Stewart in 1952 for his book *U.S. 40*. University of Wisconsin Press.

Fig. 84. The same section of U.S. 40 east of Richmond, Indiana, as shown in Fig. 83, photographed in 1980 by Thomas R. Vale and Geraldine A. Vale for their book *U.S. 40 Today*. University of Wisconsin Press.

Fig. 85. An Art Moderne Danners 5/10 store on U.S. 40 Knightstown, 1983. *IHS—Seldon Bradley.*

Fig. 86. A 1936 Studebaker President coupé, an Art Moderne streamline design. *Discovery Hall Museum, South Bend, Ind.*

Fig. 87. The Oasis Diner on U.S. 40 in Plainfield, Indiana, 1983. IHS— Seldon Bradley.

Downtown hotels dominated the lodging industry in the early twentieth century. Oriented toward railroad and public transit facilities, situated in central business districts, few hotels were automobile convenient, although some—like the Claypool (Fig. 116) in Indianapolis—attempted to accommodate motorists by providing reserved parking areas on adjacent streets. Hotels tended to emphasize public space: large entrance lobbies, lounges, restaurants, bars, banquet rooms, ballrooms, and meeting facilities. By contrast, early motels, developing out of the tradition of auto camping, tourist homes, and cabin camps, featured informal, private, even rustic spaces. Cabin camps, the immediate precursors of the motel, were private enclaves. They came in various shapes: row-on-row, L-shaped crescent, or clustered patterns. (See Figs. 43 and 44.) As cabins became more substantial, the word "cottage" crept increasingly into their naming, as did the term "court" after the 1930s.

Motels evolved by copying the linear form of cottage or motor courts and by totally integrating the room units under a single roof line in one building. Motel construction especially boomed in the 1950s and many of the now abandoned or converted structures along U.S. 40 are of this vintage. To entice travelers to spend a night, roadside entrepreneurs adorned the highway with motels in a diversity of architectural styles, with a variety of accoutrements and amenities, and, of course, with interesting names.

By the late 1950s, a number of motels had grown to be motor inns. Substantially larger and usually more luxurious, frequently with an elaborate outdoor area dominated by a swimming pool, the typical U.S. 40 motor inn also featured an expanded public space indoors. Motel chains, although not new to the industry, expanded dramatically the motor inn market. Today's dominant chains (Holiday Inns, Howard Johnson's, Quality Inns, Ramada Inns, Sheraton Inns), entering the field in the late 1950s or early 1960s, helped foster this motel form. The motel chains brought substantial regimentation to the architecture and signage of the motor inn: the above-ground archaeologist will recognize the gate house, restaurant, and room plan of the Howard Johnson's on U.S. 40 in Richmond as practically the same as the one built across the state in Terre Haute.

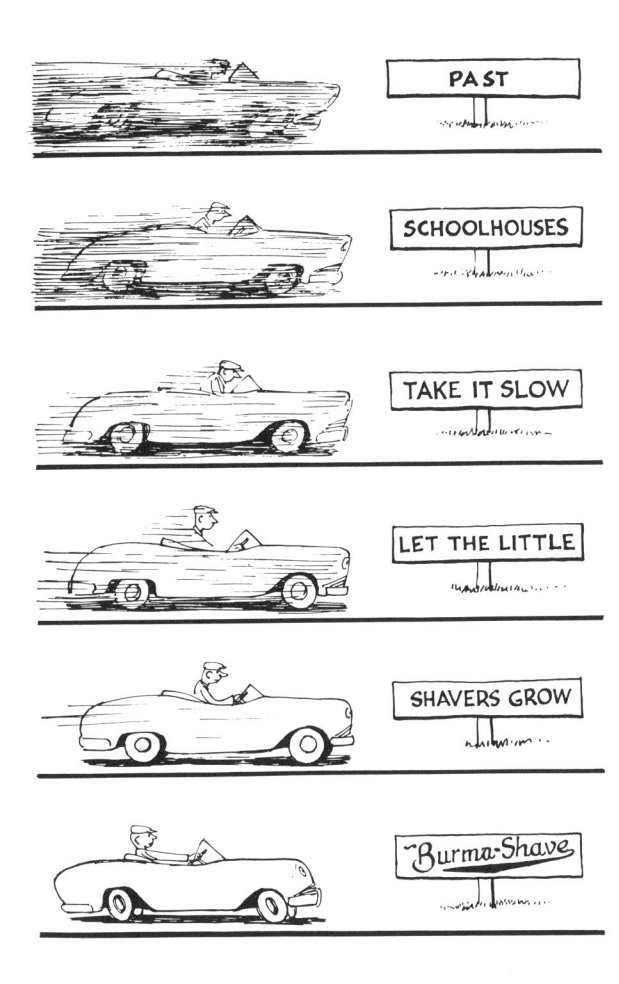

Fig. 88. Burma Shave sign sequence. From *The Verse by the Side of the Road* by Frank Rowsome, Jr. Drawings by Carl Rose. © 1965 by Frank Rowsome, Jr. Published by The Stephen Greene Press, Brattleboro, VT 05301.

In Richmond, Terre Haute, and especially in Indianapolis, we can see how the development of the American motel, in the form of the highway hotel, has come full circle in approximately fifty years. Not only has the motel penetrated the heart of the city (one chain even calls itself the "Downtowner"), but it has also grown, floor-upon-floor, to multiple-story height. Moreover, the highway hotel has expanded its services and public spaces to include all those of the traditional hotel. In turn, it might be argued that hotels such as the Hyatt Regency on U.S. 40 in downtown Indianapolis have become more motel-like, being now equipped with parking garages, large atriums simulating the informality of the out-of-doors, and often with swimming pools and other recreational facilities.

Brazil, Indiana, has its share of U.S. 40's assorted motel types, as well as many of the other artifacts representative of the road's life prior to the advent of Interstate 70. It serves, therefore, as an appropriate epitome district of the U.S. 40 era. To begin with, it is located at the beginning of one of the route's major relocations, thus making it an ideal access point to study both the pre-automotive road (eleven miles of U.S. 340 between Brazil and Terre Haute) and the "new" road of the motor highway. Brazil is also one of the towns that George Stewart, in *U.S. 40, Cross Section of the United States of America*, pointed out as typical of those found on the transcontinental highway in its route across mid-America.

U.S. 40 is Brazil's main street (Fig. 92), and its elongated business district, strung out like a long commercial ribbon from one end of the town to another, still evokes the boom years of the car culture. Commercial establishments willingly embrace the street and welcome the constant flow of road traffic. Gasoline stations, automobile dealerships, and drive-ins of all kinds abound. Brazil's downtown still suggests movement and mobility. It is a town happy about being right on the road. Even the town's exotic name suggests faraway travel, does it not?

Fig. 89. The Richmond Motel on U.S. 40 in Richmond, Indiana, 1983. *IHS—Seldon Bradley.*

Fig. 90. The Admiral Motel, 11200 East Washington Street (U.S. 40) in Indianapolis, 1983. *IHS—Seth Rossman.*

Fig. 91. The multistoried Howard Johnson's rising beyond the 1930s-style White Castle on West Washington Street (U.S. 40) in Indianapolis, 1981. *IHS— Seldon Bradley.*

A ROAD GUIDE TO U.S. 40   101

Brazil prompts us to recall a time, not all that long ago, when life moved at no more than 35 mph. Yet it also contains much evidence of the new aspects of work and play that the highway nurtured. For example, it is appropriately located close to the two major Indiana state highway patrol posts on U.S. 40 (Putnamville and Terre Haute); it is a central district for a state highway maintenance department. In close proximity are such former tourist attractions as Hoosier Highlands and Forest Park.

Interstate Highway 70: 1956-Present

By means of State Route 59, Brazil is connected to Interstate 70, one of six interstate highways that cross Indiana. The creation of Interstate 70, as a part of the 42,500-mile National System of Interstate and Defense Highways designed to link more than 90 percent of all American cities with populations over 50,000, prompted still another existence for U.S. 40. This fourth life for the road is, perhaps, the one most familiar to us, since its material manifestations are the ones that comprise our contemporary awareness of the highway environment.

The uniform red-white-blue shields and mammoth white-on-green signs of the interstate system that the landscape observer frequently sees along U.S. 40 suggest with what closeness Interstate 70 follows the general geographical orientation of the route that Jonathan Knight laid out in 1827. East of Indianapolis the interstate runs north of U.S. 40, while west of the capital city it parallels the road to the south. East of Richmond and west of Terre Haute the two highways momentarily converge, only to split apart and go their separate ways again into Ohio and Illinois, respectively. At three sites within the Indianapolis city limits, U.S. 40 intersects other components of the interstate system in Indiana: at the junctions of I-74/465, of I-70/65, and of I-465. By virtue of its central position through both Indiana and Indianapolis (desig-

Fig. 92. U.S. 40, Brazil, Indiana's main street, 1984. *IHS—Seldon Bradley.*

nated by the federal highway planners as the midwest transportation network's "hole in the donut"), U.S. 40 connects with all but three (80/90, 64, 69) of the interstate highways that crisscross the state.

What should the landscape historian make of this interaction of U.S. 40 with Interstate 70? What new road artifacts have come into existence because of Interstate 70? How has the old U.S. 40 been affected by this new highway system, the largest public works program ever undertaken in this country?

Interstate 70 looks as it does because, in part, of road surfacing and road engineering achievements first tested on federal highways such as U.S. 40. The vir-

Fig. 93. Interstate 70 and U.S. 40 signs at the intersection of the two roads just west of the Indiana-Illinois border, 1983. IHS—*Seldon Bradley*.

tues of divided arterial highways, limited access control, and improved vertical and horizontal alignments had been demonstrated prior to 1956 when the interstate system received its first major funding from the Congress. The interstate system, however, upgraded these innovations in road design, creating the highest standards appropriate for the terrain traversed and the traffic served. As a consequence, the American highway landscape took on an appearance drastically different in scale and proportion than any previous roadscape.

Consider how the interstate, as we find it paralleling U.S. 40 at places like Gem, Putnamville, and West Terre Haute, has totally changed the roadscape. In its emphasis on the *road*, it has drastically altered the *roadside*. This occurred for two reasons, both quite evident in the land use patterns surrounding the interstate. Since Interstate 70 is a highway with full control of access, this means that the usual right of owners or occupants of land abutting the highway to access, light, air, or view, is totally controlled by a public authority. County roads that suddenly dead-end at the interstate's right-of-way, long metal fences, barricades that halt potential intersecting local roads, not to mention the lack of direct commercial or residential development of the immediate interstate roadside, are the results of this federal policy.

In addition to restrictions on access, other restrictions prohibit the building of both signage and structures within a six-hundred-foot area of the interstate proper. Consequently, the style, size, and positioning of road architecture has been greatly altered, as

Cloverleaf

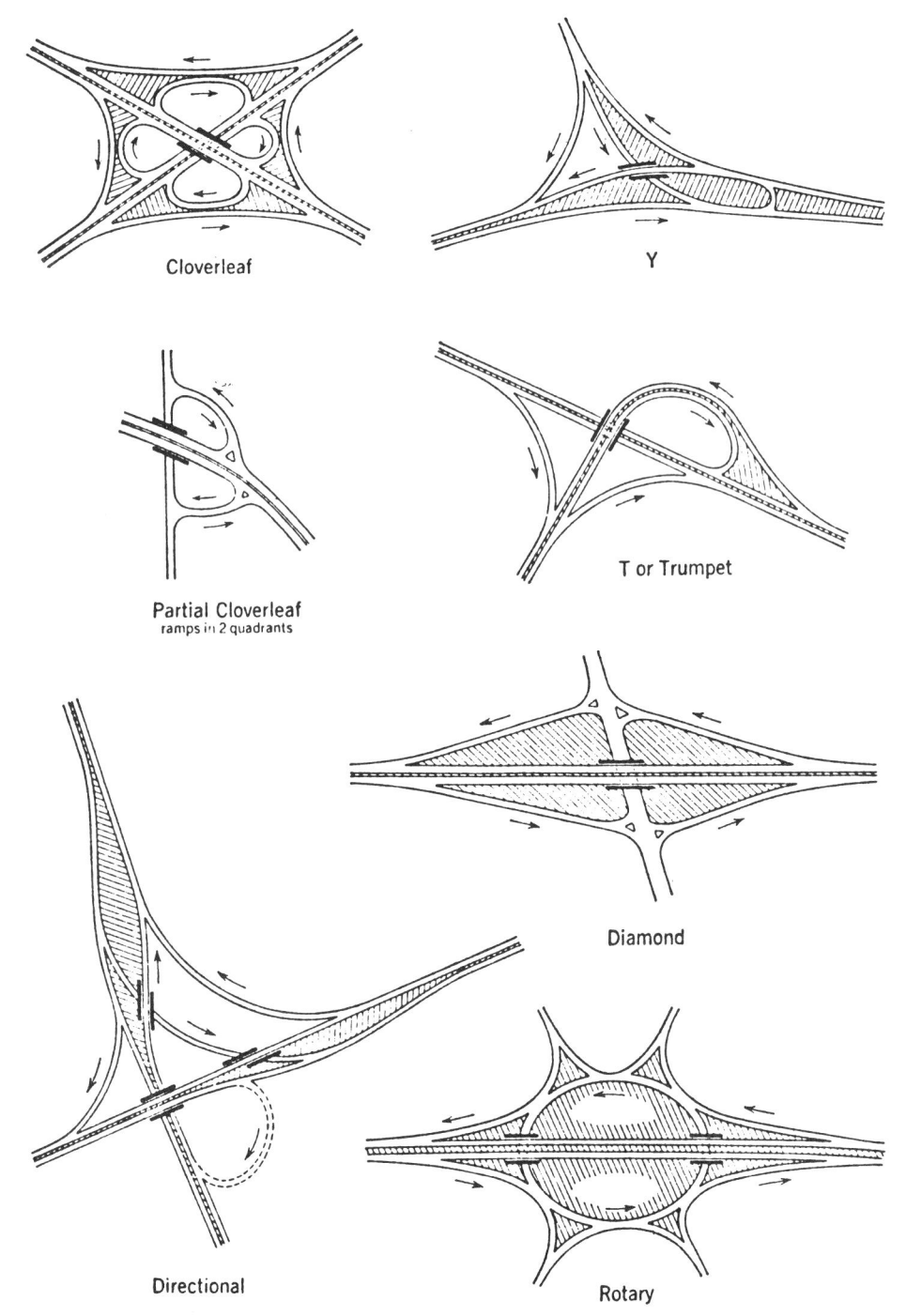

Y

Partial Cloverleaf
ramps in 2 quadrants

T or Trumpet

Diamond

Directional

Rotary

Fig. 94. Highway grade separations and interchanges. *American Association of State Highway Associations.*

Fig. 95. Old filling station on U.S. 40 cut off from access to the road when it was joined with Interstate 70 west of Terre Haute. *IHS—Seldon Bradley.*

skyscraper signs (see Fig. 96) and block-long billboards command one's attention from a distance. Some of Interstate 70's hundred-foot-high announcements for food or fuel project so far into the sky that they can be seen even from U.S. 40.

Recognizing the need to alert motorists from greater distances and traveling at faster speeds of their presence, buildings associated with the interstate (located almost exclusively at interchanges) have become nearly identical. Their message is conveyed not by their novelty but rather by their homogeneity. McDonald's golden parabolas (also identifiable on special company interstate maps) are now national landmarks of familiarity and conformity. The more vernacular graphics of the U.S. 40 roadside have been either eliminated or abstracted into bolder, simpler, corporate designs. On this nationally designed, built, and paid for (90 percent federal funds) highway, the majority of the trademarks are national. The richness of regional variety and whimsey has been largely replaced by a pervasive standardization.

Despite its apparent sameness, the interstate system still has much to teach the above-ground archaeologist. One of its novel features, the interchange, has

Fig. 96. Skyscraper sign off Interstate 70 at the Ohio/Indiana border, 1983. *IHS—Seldon Bradley.*

nurtured a new type of road life and several new artifacts. Obviously one begins with the variety in shapes and sizes of the interchanges (Fig. 94) themselves: cloverleafs, Y-forms, diamonds, T-forms, trumpets, directionals, rotaries. Where U.S. 40 and Interstate 70 conjoin in western Indiana, we discover a Y-interchange; where the two routes come together at the other end of the state, east of Richmond, we find a cloverleaf. Viewed from the air these interchanges are highway art forms and striking visual displays of modern civil engineering. Viewed from the road, they contain an extensive array of traffic-control mechanisms, drainage devices, and landscaping features (Figs. 97-100).

Clustered around most interstate highway interchanges is usually a small hamlet of gasoline stations. While most of these stations are, like the interstate itself, standardized versions of a national product, they remind us, particularly when compared with the wide assortment of other stations one still finds along U.S. 40, that this building form did not burst full-blown upon the American scene. (For the evolution of the gasoline station see Figs. 30-34.) Using the newest stations along the interchanges as benchmarks, the above-ground archaeologist can review fifty years of changing architectural and landscape tastes via gas station designs still extant on U.S. 40. For example, one can find examples of the service station as a house, often on large corner lots of what were once primarily residential thoroughfares. The addition of canopies to these small houses or cottages produced another distinctive gasoline station type in use as early as the 1920s.

The economic depression of the thirties is mirrored in the oblong box style that now enjoys a second life around the interstate exchanges, in its modern dress as a "colonialized" or "ranchified" gas station. The oblong box originally was designed to accommodate new sales efforts aimed at countering the effects of the drop in gasoline sales in the 1930s; many companies expanded auxiliary product lines, thus needing larger display rooms and larger storage spaces. Room for the sale of tires, batteries, and accessories (the so-called "TBA" line) was integrated into station design, as were offices and service bays. By the 1960s these prefabricated porcelain and plastic oblongs were phased out, and "blend-ins" (the industry's term for new styles designed to harmonize with suburban landscapes) began to appear. Complete with rustic features, such as cedar shakes, used brick, wide roof overhangs, and dark

Fig. 97. Looking west on U.S. 40 towards the intersection of U.S. 40 and Interstate 70 east of Richmond, Indiana, 1984. *IHS—Seth Rossman.*

earth color schemes, such structures are now found at many interchange sites.

The commercial archaeologist can also usually discover at such interchanges instances of the so-called "small box" station—a form with a history that goes back to earlier individually owned stations found along U.S. 40. The new "independents" of the 1960s (local jobbers and regional distributing companies who sell only gasoline and oil) often returned to the use of the canopy in their design motif. Some major oil companies continued this trend in the next decade, building, especially at interstate interchanges, stations that were little more than huge canopies (Fig. 101). Station offices were reduced to small booths (housing only an attendant and his cash register) and were located on one side of the pump islands. Restrooms and vending machines were housed in separate shedlike buildings, usually placed at one edge of the driveway. These "total canopy" stations, a return both to the original "filling station" concept of the 1910s and the house-and-canopy designs of the 1920s, were a direct result of commercial pressures generated by higher gasoline prices in an era of growing gasoline shortages.

At the State Line Truck Stop, east of Richmond off the U.S. 40 interchange of Interstate 70, the perceptive observer can see a typical gasoline pump of that

Fig. 98. Aerial view of the intersection of Interstate 70 and U.S. 40 east of Richmond, Indiana, 1976. *Indiana State Highway Commission*.

Fig. 99. Aerial view of the junction of U.S. 40 and Interstate 70 west of Terre Haute, Indiana, 1976. *Indiana State Highway Commission*.

earlier filling station era being used as a commemorative roadside symbol. And although truck stops appeared on the highway almost as quickly as did trucks, their presence is now most evident at the many interchanges along interstate routes. The contemporary truck stop is actually a miniature city, usually replete with showers, laundry, and sleeping facilities, large restaurants and coffee shops, elaborate repair garages, truck washes, and parts stores, groceries, haberdasheries, banking services, and communication facilities, including citizen band radios and close-circuit television networks.

If the modern truck stop is a true artifact of the interstate era, so is a new type of settlement morphology that the above-ground archaeologist now finds more often than not centered around an interstate

Fig. 100. Looking east from the junction of U.S. 40 and Interstate 70 west of Terre Haute, 1984. *IHS—Seth Rossman.*

Fig. 101. Century Gas station of canopy design on U.S. 40 in Plainfield, Indiana, 1983. *IHS—Seldon Bradley.*

interchange, such as the ones called Richmondville (at the east U.S. 40 interchange of I-70), Vigo Center (at the west U.S. 40 interchange of I-70), and Valley Mills (south of the U.S. 40 interchange of I-465). Historical geographer Peirce Lewis, writing about "The Unprecedented City" in *The American Land* (1979), has dubbed such areas "galactic cities." Any one of them could aptly serve as an epitome district of our own time's encounter with the American highway. As relatively new settlement patterns dependent upon abundant autos, gas, and roads, these galactic cities are dominated by shopping centers, one-story manufacturing complexes, and residential suburbs. The merchants in these areas are no longer crowded around the single downtown of a city, such as Greenfield, but are located in a far-flung shopping mall with acres of parking lot aprons. Industry no longer operates from grimy, smoke-belching, multistoried, brick mills and factories, such as those that once flourished along Richmond's river corridor. Instead, the new interchange factories are prefabricated, horizontal metal buildings, set down amidst manicured lawns, with sweeping driveways to accommodate truck transport. Scattered subdivisions make up the residential components of this contemporary but increasingly familiar landscape. In place of the old grid pattern of streets, small lots, and two- and three-story houses that we found in a highway city such as Brazil, along the interstate we find mile upon mile of houses—split-levels, California ranches, Cape Cod ramblers—spread out on acre lots set back from wide curvilinear streets. Throughout this emerging landscape complex of shopping mall, suburban factory, and automobile suburb, buildings and people are arranged in loose clusters rather like galaxies of planetary bodies, floating in space.

"Go to the edge of a midwestern county seat," recommends Peirce Lewis, "and watch the galaxy forming. There alongside the main road into town is the town shopping center. Facing a paved parking lot, and highly visible from the road, is the supermarket, windows plastered with signs for this week's special on chickens or orange juice. Across the parking lot is a discount store that sells everything from toothpaste to tires—all self-service, of course, with parking at the door." Lewis considers it significant that "the supermarket sells motor oil at a special discount price, and the discount store carries a large inventory of auto accessories and CB radios. Farther out of town is the inevitable low-slung factory that pays the wages of much of the town's workforce. Nearby, and just as inevitably, farms are being converted to small residential subdivisions."

Galactic cities now can be found springing up along much of the once-vacant countryside between U.S. 40 and the parallel route of Interstate 70. While these communities are growing, many towns and cities along U.S. 40 have suffered economic decline. The heavy volume of traffic that once flowed through places such as Straughn, Charlottesville, Harmony, Billtown, and Seelyville no longer makes its way across Indiana via U.S. 40. In bypassing such towns and their Main streets, Interstate 70 deprived them of patrons who, moving at speed limits once as high as 70 mph, were loath to get off their fast roads and venture any appreciable distance. This legacy of the interstate era is well documented in numerous now-abandoned motels, drive-ins, gasoline stations, and truck stops (Figs. 102 and 103). The U.S. 40 roadside is lined with these relics of its earlier eras. Neglected by former owners as well as the clientele that now travels on a different road, these sites will soon be the domain of the traditional archaeologist rather than the investigator who looks above-ground for his or her clues to the past.

Land Use

Chronology is a crucial tool to the archaeologist, whether working with data discovered above or below the surface. Yet, for purposes of analysis, it is also useful to investigate certain kinds of sites within broad topical frameworks. In investigating the highway, specifically U.S. 40 in Indiana, as an above-ground archaeological site, I used five such topical categories: land use, settlement patterns, road work, recreation (highway fun), and civic symbols. Questions posed by consideration of our behavior in each of these areas

Fig. 102. Abandoned gas station on U.S. 40 near Cambridge City, Indiana, 1984. *IHS—Seth Rossman.*

Fig. 103. Abandoned truck stop on U.S. 40 west of Terre Haute, 1984. *IHS— Seth Rossman.*

make the highway a useful cultural index, especially if one is interested in contemporary mores and ways of life. Answers are necessary to such questions as: How has the road affected the environment? In what ways has the road had an impact on where we live? Is the road responsible for any new occupations among us? How has the road influenced our modes of recreation? What has the road meant to us as a place for civic celebration and as a symbol of our collective identity?

Roads, no matter what their origin or type, always physically alter the environment. Highways, by definition, cannot help but make an impact on the quality of streams, hills, forests, marshlands, and rock formations they encounter as they move across the land. Monitoring the quality of this inevitable relation between the road and its environment might be done by the landscape historian, at George Stewart's suggestion in *U.S. 40*, through use of the classifications: dominating, equal, or dominated. A *dominating highway* is one which, as you drive along it, makes you more conscious of it than of the environment through which you are passing. When U.S. 40 marries Interstate 70, it becomes such a highway (see Fig. 100). The *dominated highway*, on the contrary, is one which loses its own identity because of the surroundings through which it passes. U.S. 40 is dominated, for example, when it passes along Washington Street in Indianapolis (see Fig. 104). Highways may also be dominated when they are comparatively small roads passing through high mountains or vast plains. In between these extremes lies the *equal highway*, the one which seems to be an intimate and integral part of the environment through which it passes. U.S. 40 is such a road (see Fig. 82) for much of its length in Indiana. One finds that there is a division of interest between one's focus upon the road, the roadside, and the roadscape set back from the highway.

Such a road encourages the above-ground archaeologist to be attentive to the possible impact of geology and geography upon the highway and, in turn, the highway on the environment. As U.S. 40 cuts across central Indiana, it traverses a farming area which lies between the southern hill country and the flatlands of the northern part of the state. In this fertile, gently undulating plain (Fig. 105), a traveler crosses four river systems (Whitewater, White, Blue, Wabash), passes

Fig. 104. U.S. 40 passing through Indianapolis by way of Washington Street, an example of the highway dominated by its surroundings. *IHS—Seldon Bradley.* This picture was taken with a telephoto lens.

through several major metropolitan areas, and (in its western section of Putnam, Clay, and Vigo counties) moves over a part of Indiana's clay and coal fields. This varied topography—gently rolling farmland, stretches of level prairie, river valleys, highly populated urban areas, and rugged hills—comprises what geologists call the Tipton Till Plain in the east and central part of the route and the Mitchell Plain in the west. While not as geologically or geographically diversified as either the northern or southern sections of the state, this area, nonetheless, still shows evidence, millions of years old, of its history as a glaciated plain. The evidence has been uncovered and made visible to the above-ground archaeologist traveling along U.S. 40 in various cuts and rock outcroppings, courtesy of the highway's construction.

Place-names also provide the landscape analyst with clues as to how Hoosiers have both viewed and used the land through which the highway passes. Between Richmond (selected in 1818 from several suggested names for its commendatory idea of richness of soil) and Terre Haute (a French settlement of 1720 perched on "high land"), U.S. 40 contains numerous sites whose names tell us something of their environment and how it has shaped and been shaped by those who have occupied it. Consider, for instance, Greenfield, Spring Lake, Bridgeport, Mount Meridian, Pleasant Gardens, and Cloverland—all towns located on U.S. 40.

If one expands one's purview to the counties through which the route passes, one finds many more similar environmental clues. In Clay County the towns of Coalmont, Saline City, Carbon, and Clay City all betray their origins and economic bases. The impact of the clay and limestone deposits below the earth in Putnam County becomes strikingly evident to the above-ground archaeologist in the vicinity of the Indiana State Farm. In addition to a large quarry site on the 1915 penal farm grounds that is visible from U.S. 40, one can see the shops and factories where prisoners produced brick, tile, and crushed limestone. Directly across the highway from the penal farm is the Putnamville State Police Post, a polychromatic brick building constructed of different types and hues of Indiana State Farm brick, as are several houses along this stretch of U.S. 40 that were built for prison officials and guards (Fig. 106). As one travels by the numerous quarries, strip mines, barrow pits, and slag piles in the route's western counties, one should remember how vital their products (e.g., sand, crushed rock, gravel, brick, lime) have been in creating roads such as U.S. 40. Located in the appropriately named town of Limedale in Putnam County, for example,

Fig. 105. The gently undulating terrain over which U.S. 40 passes is evident in this view of a section of the road near Knightstown, Indiana, 1983. *IHS—Seldon Bradley.* The picture was taken with a telephoto lens.

was one of the first American producers of high quality cement used in many types of road construction.

When Jonathan Knight first surveyed the route that became U.S. 40, he recorded a heavy forest cover along much of the way. Trees such as elm, walnut, hickory, sugar maple, oak, buckeye, beech, blue ash, and hackberry were abundant. Isolated natural prairie clearings were the exception rather than the rule. Today's natural environment along U.S. 40 displays a reverse ratio, with cleared land predominating and heavy timber confined to farmers' woodlots or occasional stretches allocated to a roadside park. Only by tramping along the abandoned roadbeds of the route does one get a sense of what it might have been like to travel a road through a dense forest. May T.

Watts, in her classic *Reading the Landscape of America* (1975), includes a chapter on U.S. 40 that alerts us to extant vegetation and its significance as an index to environmental change. For instance, the alert landscape historian can spot, west of Centerville, an example of "wedding" or "bride-and-groom" conifers that nineteenth-century midwestern rural folk frequently planted to mark major turning points in their own lives—a new home, a new spouse, or a new child. Communities, too, have used trees to symbolize their local pride, such as those numerous flowering crab apple trees that the residents of Knightstown have deliberately planted on both the road's east and west entrances to their community.

U.S. 40, in its east-west trek, crosses several major

Fig. 106. House on U.S. 40 near Putnamville in Putnam County, built of brick manufactured from the clay and limestone found in the area by prisoners at the nearby Indiana State Farm, 1983. *IHS—Seldon Bradley.*

watercourses on their north-south journeys to the sea. The Whitewater, the Blue, the White, and the Wabash watersheds have all been important to their regions. So have been man-made waterways, such as Indiana's short-lived canal network, of which the above-ground archaeologist on U.S. 40 turns up fragments in Terre Haute (the Wabash Canal), in Indianapolis (the Central Canal), and in Cambridge City (the Whitewater Canal). While the actual water-filled canal is still visible in Indianapolis, its evidence on the U.S. 40 route in Terre Haute is Lockport Street, and in Cambridge City a surface depression in the front lawn of homes just one-half mile south of the National Road (Fig. 107).

Crossing such natural and man-made watercourses with speed and safety necessitated certain modifications of the environment as bridges were constructed. The changing demands of higher velocity traffic and heavier vehicles further influenced bridge construction that, in turn, further altered the environment in various ways. Compare, for example, the bridges built at different times over the Whitewater River at Richmond (see Figs. 53 and 109), or compare the old bridge over Brandywine Creek east of Greenfield with the present one (Figs. 110 and 111). As a general rule, nineteenth-century bridge builders, given their traffic requirements and available construction materials, had to respect and integrate their designs with the landscape; twentieth-century planners, given their arsenal of road clearing and building technology, have tended to master and manipulate the environment.

The hand of man is also heavy on the land, if one compares the terrain needed for general overland routes, say, in the National Road era, with those in the interstate period. The specifications for the first federal road in Indiana simply stipulated that the highway was to be eighty feet in width, the timber grubbed, and the ground graded so that there would be a center track thirty to forty feet wide for traffic. By contrast, the average interstate road (Figs. 98–99) consumes approximately forty-two acres of land for each mile built. With at least four twelve-foot travel lanes, often with median strips twenty feet wide in between, and large shoulders of about thirty feet on each side, the modern twentieth-century road is an enormous land consumer. This is especially so when one realizes

Fig. 107. A fragment of the bed of the Whitewater Canal in a residential area of Cambridge City, a half mile south of U.S. 40, 1983. *IHS—Seldon Bradley.*

Fig. 108. View from Bell's Hill in Knightstown of bridge on the National Road over Montgomery's Creek, ca. 1900. *IHS.*

Fig. 109. U.S. 40 bridge over the Whitewater River in Richmond, 1984. *IHS—Seth Rossman.*

that these minimum requirements do not include the land used in the construction of feeder roads, interchanges (Fig. 112), or any of the other facets of highway engineering (e.g., viaducts, tunnels, belt lines, elevated grade crossings) usually involved when the interstate penetrates an urban area.

Settlement Patterns

U.S. 40 has had a considerable impact on how residents have occupied the middle part of Indiana. To begin with, the route cuts across three early boundary lines of settlement patterns, boundaries once agreed upon by newcomers and the native Americans after whom the state and its capital were named. In the front lawn of a McDonald's fast-food restaurant in Richmond, the landscape observer finds a stone marker detailing the 1795 Treaty of Greenville agreement with the Indians defining limits of white penetration. Farther down the highway, just at the western edge of Cambridge City, is the Twelve Mile Purchase Line of 1809; and about midway between Shady Lane and Manhattan in Putnam County we come upon still another former line of settlement, the Ten O'Clock Treaty Line.

Routes such as U.S. 40 have influenced the location of communities in at least three important ways: 1) as conduits of settlement; 2) as expanders or contractors of earlier settlements; and 3) as creators of new settlements. U.S. 40 has excellent examples of each of these patterns in landscape history.

While the road has acted as a conduit of settlement for thousands of immigrants throughout the past one hundred and fifty years, one particular migration, that of the Quakers, is clearly stamped upon the roadscape. Beginning in Richmond (whose College Avenue is believed to have the most Quakers per square foot of any street in the country) and following U.S. 40 to the West, the above-ground archaeologist has an opportunity to retrace the westward trek of many nineteenth-

Fig. 110. Bridge on the old National Road over Brandywine Creek just east of Greenfield, ca. 1900. *IHS*.

century Friends. Max Carter, director of campus ministry at Earlham College, has done just that, and a map that he has drawn shows the sites of thirty-nine Friends meetinghouses (churches) that were established adjacent to the National Road (Fig. 113). Several, such as Richmond's First Friends Church and the Plainfield Yearly Meeting, are local and architectural landmarks. As the Friends moved over the U.S. 40 route, they founded towns as well as religious congregations: Pennville (1836) and Philadelphia (1838) named after Quaker William Penn and the City of Brotherly Love that he established in Pennsylvania in 1688, as well as Greenfield (1828) and Plainfield (1839).

Knightstown (1828), of course, was named for Jonathan Knight, who, as federal surveyor of the National Road, took his assignment—"to survey the most expeditious and direct route due west from the Ohio to the Illinois border passing through the new state capitol at Indianapolis"—so literally that his road's placement was responsible for encouraging new settlements

Fig. 111. The present bridge on U.S. 40 (the old National Road) over Brandywine Creek, 1983. *IHS—Seldon Bradley*.

A ROAD GUIDE TO U.S. 40   119

Fig. 112. Cloverleaf at intersection of Shadeland Avenue and U.S. 40, on the east edge of Indianapolis, 1958. *Ray Bright, IHS.*

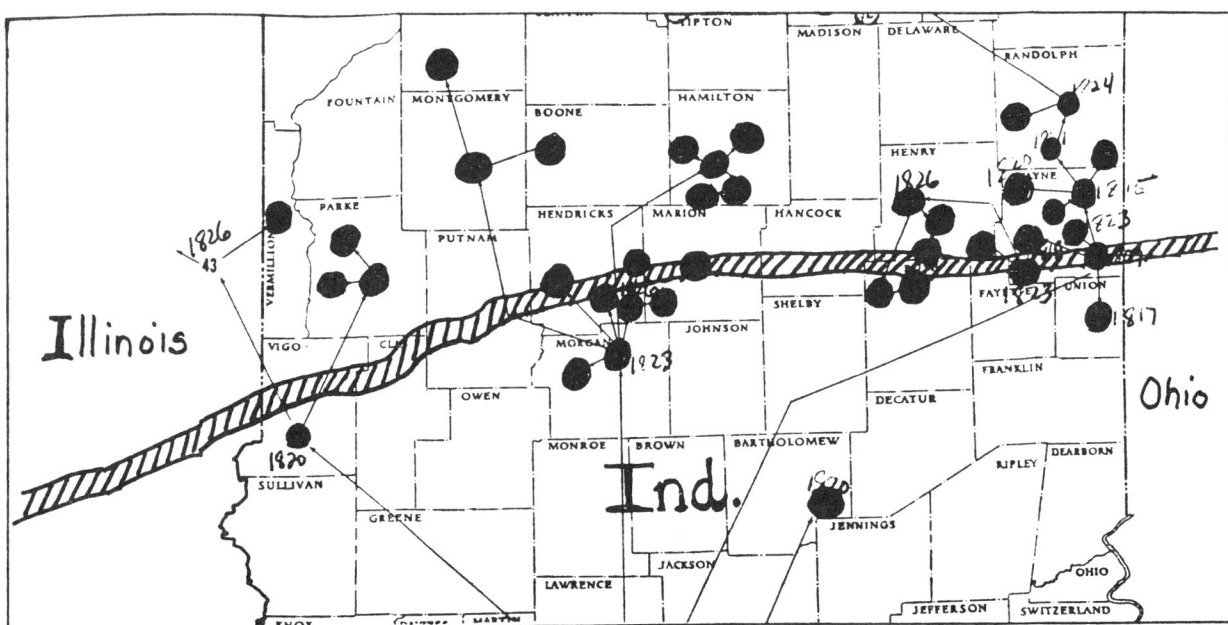

Fig. 113. Map drawn by Max Carter showing thirty-nine Friends meetings established adjacent to the National Road by early settlers. *Max Carter and Robert Lawson.*

where previously there had been none, and, conversely, in bypassing some established settlements, creating a situation which led to their atrophy if not their demise, as in the case of Salisbury and Vandalia in Wayne County, both disappearing entirely from modern maps. Only Salisbury's 1823 courthouse survives, having been located close to Centerville, a town that grew because of the road and in 1816 replaced Salisbury as the county seat. (As noted earlier, the county seat was moved to Richmond in 1873.) Knight's dedication to a straight route caused him to exclude Danville, Greencastle, and Bowling Green, the newly located seats of justice in Hendricks, Putnam, and Clay counties. Bowling Green eventually lost its county seat status to Brazil, located on U.S. 40. As we discovered earlier, Reelsville and Raysville also declined once the road was rerouted around them.

Towns such as Brazil, Richmond, Terre Haute, and Indianapolis grew enormously due to their location on the U.S. 40 route. In each of these, the road was the major overland connection linking them to the Ohio Valley to the east and the Mississippi Valley to the west. In fact, as Lee Burns has argued in *The National Road in Indiana*, the National Road drastically altered the previous immigration pattern in the state: "Practically all of the travel in Indiana before the Government road was in a condition to be used was from south to north, along the water courses and the roads and trails from Ohio, but during the next ten years a constant stream of immigration passed through Indianapolis on the National road, many of the settlers going west to the Wabash country. . . . "

The new east-west orientation that the National Road nurtured is certainly evident in Indianapolis. Here the highway, called Washington Street, bisects the city and for many years was its premier thoroughfare. A sequence of pictures (Figs. 115, 116, 117) of its intersection with Illinois Street provides a dramatic illustration of the changing roadscape of U.S. 40 in the state's largest city. Beginning as a hundred-foot-wide cattle route (it was located south of Market Street to keep the heavy traffic off the Circle), the street was soon paved with logs and populated by farm-related businesses. By the time the railroads were exerting their tremendous influence on the city in the 1860s, Washington Street had the finest shopping district in the state. An address on Washington Street was proof that one had arrived. By the turn of the century, Washington Street was a truly cosmopolitan avenue, an American "Champs-Elysees," whose storekeepers catered to customers of every taste and budget, and one could purchase there anything from feed grain to fine furniture to high fashions, from merchants whose names read like an Indianapolis "Who's Who": Ayres, Lieber, Wasson, Mayer, Strauss.

Washington Street continued as the city's preeminent shopping district until the Interstate era. It was in the 1960s that the demise of Indianapolis's main thoroughfare began. Numerous downtown establishments closed or drifted slowly away along with dwindling sales, as new settlement and commercial patterns began to evolve at large suburban shopping centers (one ironically named Washington Square, Fig. 118) located along the inner (I-70) and outer (I-465) belts of the city's interstate system. Such shopping centers served as the commercial nodes for the emerging galactic cities which are, of course, another instance of the highway's twentieth-century impact on community development and life-style.

Along Washington Street in the early 1950s, and at many other sites all along U.S. 40, appeared one other settlement pattern that has continued apace in post-World War II America: the mobile home park such as the "National Camp" community east of Indianapolis. These "wheeled suburbs" were initially a specialized manifestation of the phenomenon of personal mobility that the automobile first brought to Americans. In their manufacture, sale, and maintenance, they have since become a substantial component of the state's economy, especially in northeastern Indiana. Without

Fig. 114. Washington Street in Indianapolis in 1825, by which the old National Road would later pass through the town. *IHS*.

Fig. 115. The Bates House on the northwest corner of Washington (the old National Road) and Illinois streets in Indianapolis, 1889. *Bass Photo.*

Fig. 116. The Claypool Hotel on the site of the Bates House (Fig. 115), in 1912. Built in 1901, it was demolished in 1969. *Bass Photo.*

Fig. 117. Intersection of Washington (U.S. 40) and Illinois streets in Indianapolis, 1942. *Bretzman Collection, IHS.*

a doubt, they are a form of American shelter that has been brought into existence directly by the combination of the motor vehicle and the surfaced road. The ability to move house trailers and manufactured housing economically about the country is a function of motorized highway transportation, even if the mobile home has now become so large that it has to be hauled by truck tractor rather than the family car.

To be sure, the trailer has historical ancestors; the Conestoga wagons that rolled down the National Road were mobile homes of sorts, but definitely designed for temporary transit and far less habitable than their modern counterparts. It is interesting to note, however, that the first mass-produced trailers were built in 1933 by a Detroit firm called the Covered Wagon Company (Fig. 120). Trailers of that era were seldom more than twenty feet in length, compared with the fifty- and seventy-foot sizes common in the 1980s.

As the landscape historian investigates this recent form of American housing, once again U.S. 40 yields representative examples of its evolution from auto trailer to house trailer, to mobile home, to manufactured housing. Trailers as movable residences came into prominence during the Second World War when the government bought some thirty-eight thousand twenty-five-foot trailers to house workers in war plants located where conventional housing was in short supply. Thousands more were purchased privately for the same purpose. And the continuation of the housing shortage, then as now, has made for greater acceptance of the mobile home and its geographical setting—the mobile home park of the American highway.

Road Work

Selling new and used mobile homes and operating mobile home parks are typical occupations of men and women who, it might be said, are directly connected to the road for their livelihood. Without the road, they would have no jobs. There are many of us whom the road serves: tourists, farmers and business people shipping goods, hitchhikers, and most folk just going back and forth to their places of work. (A new feature of this latter phenomenon might be noted in the evidence of car pooling, now visible along various intersections of U.S. 40 and rural roads.) Then there are those who either serve the road directly—highway police patrols, highway department personnel, road maintenance crews (Fig. 121), or those whose services are directly dependent upon the road—teamsters, outdoor advertisers, auto dealers, and purveyors of various roadside services (Fig. 122).

Fig. 118. Washington Square, a shopping center located on the far east side of Indianapolis on East Washington Street (U.S. 40) near interstates 70 and 465, 1984. *IHS—Seldon Bradley.*

Fig. 119. Mobile home park on U.S. 40 near Pennville in Wayne County, Indiana, 1984. *IHS—Seth Rossman.*

THE NEW 1937 COVERED WAGON *Custom Coach*

WITH THE SHERMANITE STEEL BODY AND AUTOMOTIVE CHASSIS

The better to serve those who seek renowned quality coupled with elegance of interior appointments and matchless home comforts, Covered Wagon invites inspection of its latest and greatest achievement in trailer coach design — the Custom Coach.

This new 22 foot streamlined, two door tandem four wheel trailer coach now brings you the greatest triumph in modern trailer coach design — the all steel body and all steel chassis — two great Covered Wagon innovations for 1937. The new body material known as Shermanite consists of a galvannealed steel inseparably combined with plywood to give you a material 55% lighter than automobile body steel — rustproof — shock-proof — and 100 times more dent-proof than steel itself. It is many times more impervious to heat and cold than either steel or aluminum and is 22 times more rigid.

Don't fail to inspect the Covered Wagon Custom Coach at your nearest dealer or see **all** the new interior features of these Covered Wagon **All Steel** trailers at your Automobile Show. Post yourself on Covered Wagon values. Write for new literature. New low time payment plan.

**3 Models, $395 and up F.O.B. Factory.
Easy Terms for Your Convenience.**

COVERED WAGON
479 Cass Avenue, Mt. Clemens, Mich.

ORIGINATORS AND WORLD'S LARGEST TRAILER COACH BUILDERS
Please Mention TRAILER TRAVEL *In Writing Advertisers*

Fig. 120. Advertisement for the Covered Wagon Custom Coach

COVERED WAGON introduces this SENSATIONAL trailer coach value

The STANDARD at $495 F.O.B. FACTORY

The ideal low cost trailer coach equipped for cross continent travel vacationing and camping. Accommodates four.

THIS new 17-foot overall Standard Model brings you beyond question the greatest all-time trailer coach value ever offered for the price. All-steel chassis with six-inch frame — Shermanite Steel body — special spring-steel drawbar — exclusive, patented, railroad type coupler and a host of other brilliantly designed interior and exterior fixtures and appointments. This achievement in modern trailer coach design includes clothes lockers—a kitchen unit with pantry, cabinets, drawers, sink, running water, work table and ice box — cooking stove, electric lights, double bed, dining nook and numerous other home-like comforts created for utility and beauty. Visit your nearest dealer and carefully appraise the construction, design and fittings of this new Covered Wagon —compare it with any other trailer coach in this new low price range.

There are four models from which to choose—all available on new low time payment plan. Write for illustrated literature — or send 10c postage for new four-color Trailer Book.

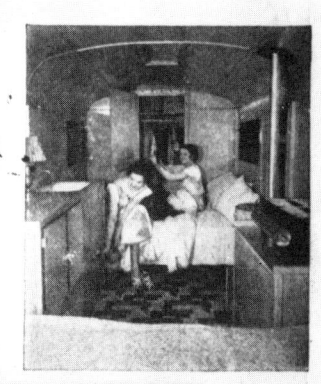

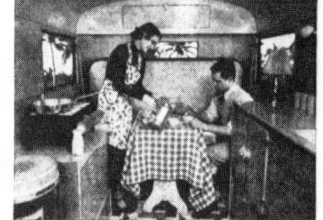

Looking forward showing davenport bed — large wardrobe and lockers. The kitchen unit is complete with all accessories.

With double davenport bed made up. Note double bed in foreground to sleep two more

The dining nook is attractively arranged to seat four or five at mealtime.

COVERED WAGON CO., 538 Cass Avenue, Mt. Clemens, Mich.

COVERED WAGON TRAILER HOMES
ORIGINATORS AND WORLD'S LARGEST BUILDERS
TRAVEL BY COVERED WAGON ... AND SAVE.

and Trailer Homes, 1937. *Detroit Historical Society.*

These two categories of road people contain those among us who both make the road work and who work the road. We already have examined much of the material culture evidence of their toil in our analysis of their gasoline stations, motels, and restaurants. Are there any other distinctive artifacts or landscape features by which we might also know these people and their increasing influence in contemporary culture?

Consider, as you drive U.S. 40, the variety of business and social functions that can be performed without leaving your car; that is, the pervasiveness of "drive-in" facilities in which people work along the roadscape. It is possible to leave and pick up laundry and cleaning, make deposits and withdrawals at banks, pick up a grocery order (Fig. 123), see a movie, borrow books, buy stamps, pay taxes, go to church, pay traffic fines, eat breakfast, lunch, and dinner without getting out of one's car. And, of course, some entrepreneurs work right out of their car or truck or van. From the earliest peddlers and street merchants (Fig. 124) to today's traveling salesmen, the highway has always been a place for doing business. So it is also for bus drivers, auto insurance adjusters, and taxi drivers.

As the above-ground archaeologist quickly realizes, many businesses are where they are because of where the highway is located. An airport such as the Indianapolis International was deliberately sited as it was by city planners so as to be accessible to U.S. 40 at Ben Davis. The direction of the interstate system is, of course, now determining where many of us work. The mammoth consolidated school buildings that have replaced the one-room township schools are so situated because they need to be serviced by school buses, whose manufacturers (e.g., the Wayne Works in Richmond), one should also note, derive their work from the road. In similar fashion, workers at the Great Dane Trucking Company on U.S. 40 build vehicles that provide jobs for teamsters and truckers. The District Highway Department in Greenfield and the State Highway Commission in Indianapolis are employers because of the road. So are work places such as license bureaus and traffic courts, and organizations such as the Hoosier Motor Club.

In addition to the artifacts of specific road work sites, like bus stations, mechanic garages, car rental lots, and highway police posts, one should not forget

Fig. 121. Men at work repairing the U.S. 40 bridge over the Wabash River west of Terre Haute, Indiana, 1983. *IHS—Seldon Bradley.*

Fig. 122. Patrons at Jim's Car Wash in Richmond, Indiana, 1983. *IHS—Seldon Bradley.*

that the route has also been filled, from time to time, with the sites and structures of other work life that have been important throughout American labor and economic history. These include work places devoted to extracting mineral resources (such as the strip mines in Clay County); to producing energy (e.g., the Terre Haute Pumping Station); to business and industry (e.g., the one-time Duesenberg auto plant in Indianapolis or the Eli Lilly Laboratory in Greenfield); to the development of agricultural resources (such as the region's famous nursery plots in Wayne County or the dairy and hog/corn farms of central Indiana).

Since U.S. 40 makes much of its way through rural Indiana, the route reflects a history of changing human activities, relations, and values in the ways that people have farmed the land. Most of the route's agricultural landscape—its structures as well as its patterned acres of production—evolved during the last half of the nineteenth century. So did the artifacts (e.g., creameries, trackside elevators, canneries, feed mills, co-op stores) that we find in the market towns and trading centers along the road and which are part of the support system of an agricultural economy. In the past eighty years, however, new machinery and new structures have streamlined agriculture, allowing larger and fewer farms and thus accounting, in part, for the number of abandoned farmhouses (Fig. 126) that one also finds along U.S. 40. Faster transport, better roads, and new farming techniques have led, ironically, to both greater diversity and more specialization. New sources (and shortages) of energy, new kinds of building materials (metal pole barns replacing heavy timber barns, Fig. 127), hybrid crops (marked by field demonstration plots), and exotic chemicals (visible in the yards of implement dealers) have greatly changed the farm economy as well as its landscape. The new horizontal emphasis of this contemporary agricultural landscape (one-story ranch style farmhouse and low, identical metal sheds for animals or machinery) is quickly replacing the more vertical, multistory, pyramid-roofed cube farmhouses and mammoth gambrel- and rainbow-roofed barns of the past.

From the road, the above-ground archaeologist can spot other changes and features of the old and new in farm work. For example, in addition to monitoring farmhouse types (ranging from Gothic Revival houses to double-wide mobile homes) and barns (hay barns, dairy barns, loafing barns), one should be on the lookout for summer kitchens, smokehouses, granaries,

Fig. 123. Drive-up grocery in Richmond, Indiana, 1983. *IHS—Seldon Bradley.*

Fig. 124. Street vendor on Washington Street (the old National Road) in Indianapolis, ca. 1894. *IHS.*

Fig. 125. Lost Creek Elementary School on U.S. 40 east of Terre Haute, 1984. *IHS—Seth Rossman.*

chicken houses, corncribs (wood, wire mesh, aluminum), silos (wood, masonry, glass-lined, bunker), milkhouses and milking parlors, machinery sheds, farrowing houses, and outdoor privies. Along the rural countryside, we also encounter sites and structures important to the collective life of Indiana farm families: rural churches and cemeteries, schools, county homes, township and grange halls, and county fair sites.

Recreation—Highway Fun

U.S. 40 currently brings visitors to numerous county fairs along its route, as well as to the annual state fair in Indianapolis. In so doing, it fulfills another of its many cultural roles: bringing enjoyment into our lives. This recreational function of the highway has especially expanded in the twentieth century, as Americans have had more leisure time to spend on the road. The use of the road as a place to play (or as a way to get to other playgrounds) has taken many forms both on the road and along the roadside.

At first, simply touring by bicycle (Fig. 129) or in an open auto was a great sport in and of itself, a tradition that continues in present-day outings of motorcyclists, auto club tours, and vintage car rallies. Going out for a quiet Sunday afternoon drive with family or friends also became a ritual form of relaxation once the automobile was accessible to most middle-class Americans. "Cruising" was the teenage counterpart of this custom, usually practiced on Friday or Saturday nights. By the mid-1920s, however, Americans got very serious about having fun on and alongside the road. Resorts, like Hoosier Highlands or Hi-Way Springs, state parks, and campgrounds came into existence. Amusement parks like Wonderland Park in Indianapolis (Fig. 130) were located right on U.S. 40. Roadside attractions provided thrill-seekers with en-

Fig. 126. Abandoned farmhouse on U.S. 40 near Philadelphia in Hancock County, Indiana, 1984. *IHS—Seth Rossman.*

tertainment ranging from simple rest stops and quiet woodland retreats to demolition derbies and speed trials at the National Drag Strip in Ohio.

Unfortunately, the two roadside parks established by the state along U.S. 40 are now only of use to above-ground archaeologists. One, just east of Stilesville, is fenced in, overgrown with weeds, and totally off limits to travelers who might seek its delightful shade. The other, located at a spring east of Knightstown (Fig. 131), has satisfied the thirst of thousands of passersby since the origin of the National Road, but now has been condemned by the state board of health. The rustic stone well site built by the Works Progress Administration during the New Deal still stands, but health inspectors claim that the natural water does not meet their standards. A posted injunction that "It Isn't Safe To Drink The Water" seems to be disregarded with total impunity by both locals and transients. In addition to these two roadside parks, there are many others along the route that suggest our changing views of recreation, park design, and land use. Dresser Memorial Park stretches along both sides of U.S. 40 in Terre Haute and is dedicated to the memory of Paul Dresser (1857-1906), composer of the Indiana state song, "On the Banks of the Wabash." At the opposite end of the state in Richmond there is Glen Miller Park (Fig. 132), and, in between, one finds the Lewisville City Park, Crietz Park in Cambridge City, and Riley Memorial Park in Greenfield, where flows the Brandywine Creek (source of

132 U.S. 40: A ROADSCAPE OF THE AMERICAN EXPERIENCE

Fig. 127. Modern pole barn and old timber barn on U.S. 40 between Greenfield and Philadelphia, Indiana, 1984. *IHS—Seth Rossman.*

Fig. 128. Hancock County, Indiana, fair on grounds a half mile off the old National Road, ca. 1900. *IHS.*

J. W. Riley's poem on the "Old Swimming Hole"). In Indianapolis, the U.S. 40 traveler has his pick of Willard and White River Park.

Museums of all types also line the route. One local organization, the Clay County Historical Society, tells its story to visitors in a Beaux Arts building that was formerly a post office. Historic house museums, such as the Riley Homestead (Greenfield) and the Huddleston House (Cambridge City), are everywhere, their vogue as a mode of museum interpretation dating back to the beginning of widespread auto touring in the 1920s. Appropriately enough, there is an Early Auto Museum right on Wabash Avenue in Terre Haute. Several storefront museums can be found, as well as numerous museums of erotica—Indiana's way of presenting pornography, since state laws stipulate a dealer in such materials must call his establishment a museum.

Local sideshows, "Indian" trading posts, exotic gift shops, and supposedly one-of-a-kind roadside attrac-

A ROAD GUIDE TO U.S. 40   133

Fig. 129. Two friends setting out for a bicycle tour from Woodruff Place, a mile north of East Washington Street (the old National Road) in Indianapolis, 1912. *Louise Carpenter Stanfield Collection, IHS.*

Fig. 130. Wonderland Park on the southwest corner of East Washington (the old National Road) and Gray streets in Indianapolis, ca. 1910. *Indiana State Library.*

Fig. 131. Knightstown Spring on U.S. 40 east of Knightstown, Indiana, ca. 1940. *Marsha Mullin.*

Fig. 132. Entrance to Glen Miller Park on U.S. 40 in Richmond, Indiana. *IHS— Seth Rossman.*

tions where one can see such wonders as "The World's Largest Snake" are no longer as prolific as they once were. Nor are the souvenir shops that provided travelers with post cards, games, toys, glassware, ashtrays, handicrafts, china, coin banks, and miscellaneous oddities to take home to friends and relatives who did not have the fun of being part of a road trip. If one was so unfortunate as to have been left at home, one could, of course, vicariously play on the road. Once upon a time no toy box was complete without a model service station and an ample supply of cars and trucks. Adults also enjoyed road fun, playing card games such as "Touring," first introduced in 1926, and any number of other auto-race parlor board games.

Of course, *the* premier auto race in America actually takes place right off U.S. 40 around Memorial Day at the Indianapolis 500 (Fig. 133). In a community called Speedway, with streets named Firestone, Fisher, Auburn, Cord, and Hulman, are all the artifacts of competitive racing: the two-and-a-half mile rectangular track known as "the Brickyard," a museum of racing memorabilia, and motels to handle Speedway visitors, plus all the accoutrements of an international week-long civic festival that celebrates the road and those who can drive the fastest on it for a 500-mile marathon.

Since the first five-hundred mile race was run in 1911, crowds have jammed Indianapolis to watch drivers compete at speeds starting at 74.59 mph (average speed of winner Ray Harroun of the Marmon Company of Indianapolis in 1911) and now topping out at speeds in excess of 200 mph. Beginning in 1957, the race became part of a three-day festival sponsored by an organization of Indianapolis businessmen, including a golf tournament, a mayor's breakfast, a governor's ball, the inevitable 500 Queen, and a street parade. Should the above-ground archaeologist come anywhere near the Speedway site in mid-May, during the two weeks of time trials or during "Race Week" prior to the Memorial Day holiday, he or she is likely to witness a civic celebration of colossal proportions: college and high school bands practicing, the public feting of famous racers, the ceremonial appearances of visiting celebrities—all in preparation for an event that now far surpasses the Indiana State Fair in national publicity.

Civic Symbols

Memorial Day is celebrated differently in most other U.S. 40 route towns in Indiana than in Indianapolis with its "500" festivities. The highway is filled with picnickers en route to parks, resorts, and other holiday areas as summer officially begins. In many

Fig. 133. Lineup for the first Indianapolis 500 in 1911. *Bretzman Collection, IHS.*

Fig. 134. Circus parade on the old National Road in Greenfield, Indiana, ca. 1910. *IHS.*

communities, U.S. 40 as Main Street is also the scene of local parades honoring the war dead of American history. In this context, the highway serves a final function of which the landscape historian should be cognizant. The highway has been (and continues to be) an important public stage on which we enact a variety of civic pageants, symbolic of both the triumphs and the tensions of our communal life. For example, consider how many parades have been held in U.S. 40 communities commemorating the nation's birthday each July 4. Think of how often, beginning with the Mexican War in 1844 and most recently with Vietnam, the route has been a thoroughfare where Hoosiers marched off to war and then paraded again upon returning home. In fact, after the Second World War, the route in Richmond was even designated as a Blue Star Memorial Highway, a way of honoring those men and women who died in the service of their country. And, of course, there have also been other parades: the arrival of the nineteenth-century chautauqua or minstrel troupe in town; the colorful entry of the circus; or the triumphal return of a local high school team after having achieved some exhalted degree of "Hoosier Hysteria." In 1976, U.S. 40 was chosen as part of the route that the bicentennial National Wagon Train took in its trek across Indiana.

The observer of U.S. 40 will also note that this highway has been a public platform where unpopular causes have had their say. Dissidents joining Coxey's Army to protest the federal government's failure to alleviate the economic conditions of the Panic of 1893 made their way to Washington along the former National Road. So did the "Bonus Marchers" of post-World War I in their attempt to lobby for congressional approval of veterans' benefits. In 1979, the United Grain Farmers of America could be seen making their Tractor Drive to Washington. The road has been the rallying ground of the Ku Klux Klan, striking workers, and protesting students. On its civic stage, American wars have been both celebrated and condemned.

The road has often hosted celebrations of itself. In the 1920s and 1930s, many towns along the route celebrated its centennial during "National Road Days." The National Road Museum in Zanesville, Ohio, is dedicated to recounting the historic role of "the Main

Fig. 135. The Rainbow Division returning from World War I, marching north on Meridian Street from its intersection with Washington Street (the old National Road) to Monument Circle in Indianapolis, May 7, 1919. *Bass Photo.*

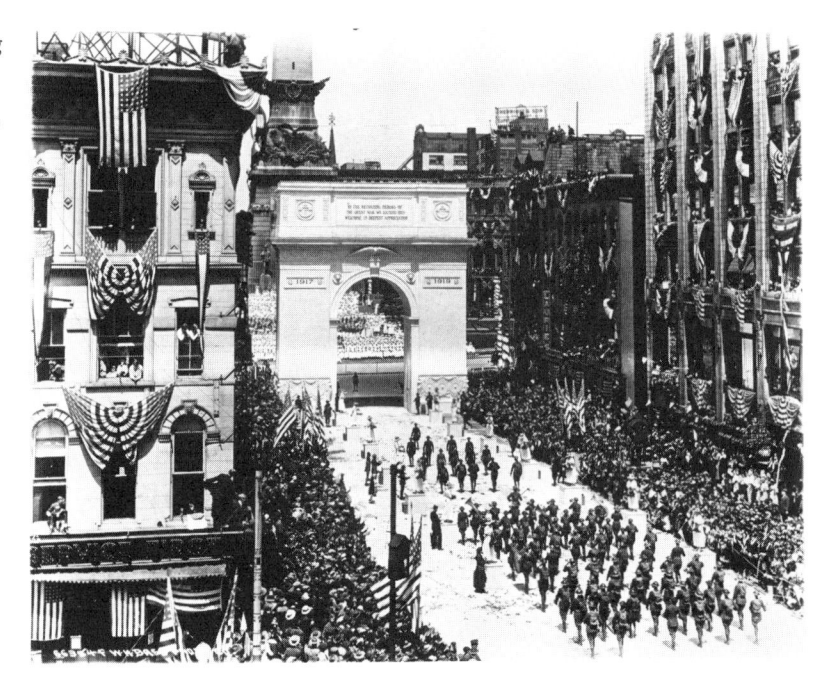

Fig. 136. Grand Army of the Republic parade on Washington Street (the old National Road) in Indianapolis, 1920. *Bass Photo.*

Fig. 137. Boat show on Wabash Avenue (U.S. 40) in Terre Haute in 1956. *Martin Collection, IHS.*

Fig. 138. Streetcar strike at the corner of Washington (the old National Road) and Pennsylvania streets, 1893. *IHS.*

Fig. 139. Tractors on Washington Street in Indianapolis during the farmers march on Washington, D.C., 1979. *Charles A. Robinson.*

Fig. 140. Indians marching from California to Washington, D.C., in protest of nuclear development on Indian land, 1980. *Frank Espich.*

Fig. 141. Wayne County Courthouse on U.S. 40 in Richmond, Indiana, 1984. The structure in the foreground is part of the municipal complex and is partially underground. *IHS—Seldon Bradley*. This picture was taken with a telephoto lens.

Street of America," while historic preservationists in eastern Indiana promote it via maps that proclaim it as the state's "Corridor of History."

Local events and hometown life are also frequently symbolized on U.S. 40. Street fairs of the present recall similar celebrations of the past. Community centennials and other local history anniversaries, as well as numerous regional festivals (e.g., Whitewater Days in Cambridge City), invariably spill over onto the highway in some form or another. An everchanging marquee of formal and informal signage along the route alerts the road denizen to these local cultural events. Local culture even comes in the form of political ribbon cutting whenever a new section or interchange of Interstate 70, connecting or diverting traffic from U.S. 40, is opened.

Politicians have long recognized the symbolic power of certain civic spaces along the road—Monument Circle and its Meridian Street intersection in Indianapolis or the great courthouse squares in Richmond, Greenfield, Indianapolis, Brazil, and Terre Haute (Figs. 141-45). Incidentally, the courthouses in these road towns form a useful index across time of public architecture, ranging from Centerville's one-time 1823 log structure to Richmond's 1970 partially-underground municipal facility.

In Richmond, we can also see an example of contemporary urban planning in that city's novel reuse of U.S. 40 following a local disaster. In April, 1968, a dreadful explosion totally leveled two downtown city blocks and spread destruction over a fourteen-block area, killing forty-one persons and injuring over one hundred. The multimillion dollar blast, apparently set off by gas leaks and gun powder stored in a sporting goods store, prompted an instant need for re-urbanization. Over the next decade, the ten-block area east of the Whitewater River was reshaped into a new retail and governmental complex. U.S. 40 was re-routed with the state's permission, and part of its former route through the heart of Richmond became a four-block-long pedestrian mall. Completed in 1972, the Richmond Promenade (Fig. 146) is a corridor of greenery, fountains, and benches of award-winning design. Downtown shoppers now walk daily over a

A ROAD GUIDE TO U.S. 40   141

Fig. 142. Hancock County Courthouse on U.S. 40 in Greenfield, Indiana, 1984. *IHS—Seth Rossman*.

Fig. 143. The old Marion County Courthouse on East Washington Street (U.S. 40) in Indianapolis just before its demolition in 1960. The new City-County Building rises behind it. *Bass Photo*.

Fig. 144. Clay County Courthouse on U.S. 40 in Brazil, Indiana, 1984. *IHS—Seth Rossman.*

Fig. 145. Vigo County Courthouse at the intersection of U.S. 40 and U.S. 41 in Terre Haute, Indiana, 1984. *IHS—Seth Rossman.*

Fig. 146. Promenade in Richmond, Indiana, a pedestrian mall built in 1972 over U.S. 40 which was rerouted after the area was ravaged by a gas explosion in April, 1968. *Indianapolis News — George Telford.*

portion of local history that has been, successively, the National Road, the Wayne County Turnpike, the city's Main Street, the National Old Trails Road, and U.S. 40.

The U.S. 40 Route as an Above-Ground Archaeological Site

Thus has the U.S. 40 route continued to evolve. Itself springing from something that already existed, it has always also continued to change. Sometimes it changes so quickly that its landscape shifts within a single day, even within the few hours it takes to drive from Indianapolis to Terre Haute and return. Some of its features, explored so recently in this particular above-ground archaeological investigation, will have been obliterated or drastically altered before this book is even published. New artifacts will have appeared. Each time I have explored the highway, I have found it to have changed slightly at various points along its route. Thus, the road is a special type of material culture evidence; it is a huge artifact assemblage that is, literally, always on the move. By definition it lacks, and always will lack, the logical and complete unity of anything that is created by a single impulse, such as the billboards, farmhouses, or bridges that form its individual parts. In its course from Richmond to Terre Haute, the highway sometimes swerves for geographical reasons because of the natural environment, but it also sometimes takes a different path due to economic or political pressures. Such pressures may no longer be operative, but the highway continues to run where it previously ran because of such historical factors.

In short, U.S. 40 in Indiana is a linear palimpsest of a large segment of the state's past. It touches long-established cities, most of which were founded before 1850. It crosses rich farmlands, mining regions, and industrial centers. It is a highway on which, if one looks carefully, one can see layer upon layer of past and present evidence of our settlement patterns, of how we have used the natural environment, as well as many of the forms of our work and play. U.S. 40 is a cross section of our culture, an outdoor museum of the ways we were and are.

III The Road in American Life—Selected Resources

Every historiographer or bibliographer quickly realizes the enormous difficulty of his task, no matter how specialized his topic. I have definitely found this to be the case in my attempt here both to suggest valuable studies that I consulted on the U.S. 40 route as an individual highway and also to include noteworthy research on the more general topic of the historical role of the road in American life.

What follows is a list of works for studying both of these topics. It is meant to help readers who may wish to pursue further some of the topics I have discussed, to suggest the kinds of documentary material on which I have relied in my research, and to indicate my heavy debt to other scholars. But it is not a complete bibliography on any aspect of the subject, nor does it include all the works I have used. After a brief general section, the remainder of the bibliography follows the narrative sequence of topics which I have presented in Parts I and II of this volume.

Reading the Road: The Above-Ground Archaeology of the American Highway

I have always been pleased, given my strong interest in state and local history, that my earliest attempt to articulate my concept of "above-ground archaeology" first appeared under the title, "Above-Ground Archaeology: Discovering a Community's History through Local Artifacts" in *Local History Today* (1979), edited by Thomas K. Krasean and published by the Indiana Historical Society. This initial statement of my approach to studying the built environment as a historical resource was later expanded as chapter nine of my volume, *Artifacts and the American Past* (Nashville, Tenn.: American Association for State and Local History, 1980).

Three standard histories of the American highway are vital to anyone seeking an overview of the topic: George R. Taylor, *The Transportation Revolution* (New York: Rinehart & Co., 1951); Jean Labatut and Wheaton J. Lane (eds.), *Highways in Our National Life, A Symposium* (Princeton, N. J.: Princeton University Press, 1950), and Albert C. Rose, *Historic American Roads: From Frontier Trails To Superhighways* (New York: Crown Publishers, 1976). Likewise, three highly interpretive volumes have been useful to my conceptualization of road in the American experience: Lewis Mumford, *The Highway and the City* (New York: Harcourt, Brace and World, 1963); John B. Rae, *The Road and the Car in American Life* (Cambridge, Mass.: The MIT Press, 1971); and George W. Pierson, *The Moving American* (New York: Knopf, 1973). In addition to the bibliographies found in all of these works, I would recommend chapter 8, "Roads, Streets, and Highways" in *Public Works History in the United States*, compiled and edited by Suellen M. Hoy and Michael

C. Robinson (Nashville, Tenn.: American Association for State and Local History, 1981), pp. 215-67.

In my discussion of early road typology, I have relied on Philip P. Mason's succinct *A History of American Roads* (Chicago: Rand McNally, 1967) and especially his *The League of American Wheelmen and the Good Roads Movement, 1880-1905* (Ann Arbor: University of Michigan Press, 1958). I think J. Todd Snow is on to something in his claims for "The 'New Road' in the United States: Spatial and Behavioral," *Landscape*, XVII, No. 1 (Autumn, 1967), pp. 13-16, emerging at the end of the nineteenth century. Snow's analysis is bolstered by Roland Rainer, "Space and the Modern Highway," *Landscape*, II, No. 3 (Spring, 1953), pp. 2-7, and Robert Capot-Rey, "Rails into Highways," *Landscape*, II, No. 2 (Autumn, 1952), pp. 8-13.

On the development of parkways, I would recommend the work of Clay McShane, "American Cities and the Coming of the Automobile, 1870-1910" (Ph.D. dissertation, University of Wisconsin, 1975); on early freeways, see David Brodsley, *L. A. Freeway, An Appreciative Essay* (Berkeley: University of California Press, 1981), and on interstates, Mark H. Rose's *Interstate: Express Highway Politics: 1941-1956* (Lawrence: Regents Press of Kansas, 1979). Robert A. Caro's mammoth biography of Robert Moses—*The Power Broker: Robert Moses and the Fall of New York* (New York: Vintage Books, 1975)—is superb on one of the country's most influential road builders. Carl Condit's two-volume *American Building Art* (New York: Oxford University Press, 1960-61) is useful on many aspects of the history of highway engineering. The historical photography found in Charles W. Wixom's *Pictorial History of Roadbuilding* (Washington, D.C.: American Roadbuilder Association, 1975) is also worth reviewing.

Above-ground archaeologists are, understandably, much taken with bridges. In addition to the primer that T. Allan Comp and Donald Jackson have prepared, titled *Bridge Truss Types: A Guide to Dating and Identifying* (American Association for State and Local History Technical Leaflet 95, *History News*, XXXII, No. 5, May, 1977), I have consulted David Plowden, *Bridges, The Spans of North America* (New York: The Viking Press, 1974), George E. Gould, *Indiana Covered Bridges through the Years* (Indianapolis: Indiana Covered Bridge Society, 1977), and H. J. Hopkins, *A Span of Bridges* (New York: Praeger, 1970). As an above-ground archaeological exercise, David Weitzman's "A Conversation with Bridge 3," *Historic Preservation*, XXXI, No. 5 (Nov.-Dec., 1979), pp. 11-17, is an excellent example.

Information about road surfaces can be found in Clay McShane, "Transforming the Use of Urban Space: A Look at the Revolution in Street Pavements, 1880-1924," *Journal of Urban History*, V, No. 3 (May, 1979), pp. 279-307; Carole Rifkind, *Main Street; The Face of Urban America* (New York: Harper and Row, 1977); and J. G. James, "50 Years of White Lines," *Roads and Road Construction*, XLII (1964), pp. 409-414. In this context, Chapter 2, "Roads," in the U. S. Department of Transportation's *A Nation in Motion: Historic American Transportation Sites* (Washington, D.C.: U. S. Government Printing Office, 1976), will alert the above-ground archaeologist to important roadway artifacts around the country. In order to know more about the "roads" under our roads, I can recommend Stanley K. Schultz and Clay McShane, "To Engineer the Metropolis: Sewers, Sanitation, and City Planning in Late-Nineteenth-Century America," *Journal of American History*, LXV, No. 2 (Sept., 1978), pp. 389-411. For learning the historical significance of what grows alongside the road, May T. Watts, *Reading the Landscape of America* (Rev. ed. New York and London: Macmillan, 1975) is invaluable for deciphering the natural history of the roadside, a practice I attempted to nurture in chapter 7, "Vegetation as Historical Data: A Historian's Use of Plants and Natural Material Culture Evidence," in *Artifacts and the American Past*, pp. 147-59.

Street-name history remains a major area of needed research in the study of the American road. Two studies on city streets worthy of imitation are: Robert I. Alotta, *Street Names of Philadelphia* (Philadelphia: Temple University Press, 1975) and Henry Moscow, *The Street Book: An Encyclopedia of Manhattan's Street Names and Their Origins* (New York: Hagstrom Company, 1978). While it does not specifically focus on individual street names of towns and cities, Ronald Baker and Marvin Carmony's *Indiana Place Names* (Bloomington: Indiana University Press, 1975) is the best reference resource on the subject in the state. Two delightful lexicons by Stuart Berg Flexner contain much information on the historical usage of road nomenclature: *I Hear America Talking* (New York: Van Nostrand Reinhardt, 1976), and *Listening To America* (New York: Simon and Schuster, 1982).

Inasmuch as roads come by many shapes as well as many names, I have used Grady Clay, *Alleys: A Hidden Resource* (Louisville: Grady Clay and Co., 1978) and James Borchert, *Alley Life in Washington* (Urbana, Ill.: University of Illinois Press, 1980) to understand this neglected feature of the built environment. On "Main Streets," see two essays by Richard V. Francaviglia, "Main Street USA," *Landscape*, XXI, No. 3 (Spring/Summer, 1977), pp. 18-22 and "Main Street Revisited," *Places*, I, No. 3 (Oct., 1974), pp. 7-11.

On public art, outdoor murals, civic sculpture, and street furniture, there has been a growing literature. Most helpful to me have been Ronald Lee Fleming and Renata von Tscharner, *Place Makers: Public Art that Tells You Where You Are* (New York: Hastings House, 1981); Marianne Doezema and June Hargrove, *The Public Monument and Its Audience* (Cleveland: Cleveland Museum of Art, 1977); Eva Cockcroft *et al.*, *Toward a People's Art: The Contemporary Mural Movement* (New York: E. P. Dutton, 1977); James M. Goode, *The Outdoor Sculpture of Washington, D.C.: A Comprehensive History Guide* (Washington, D.C.: Smithsonian Press, 1974); Sally Henderson and Robert Landau, *Billboard Art* (San Francisco: Chronicle Books, 1981); and Mimi and Robert Melnick, "Manhole Covers: Artifacts in the Streets," *California Historical Quarterly*, XL, No. 4 (Winter, 1976), pp. 352-63.

The broad history of electrification of American streets and roads has been traced by Kate Bolton, "The Great Awakening of the American Night," *Landscape*, XXIII, No. 3 (Autumn, 1979), pp. 41-47, while Sara Noreen has explored the story in a single city: *Public Illumination in Washington, D.C.: An Illustrated History* (Washington, D.C.: George Washington University, 1975). The often-forgotten (in a double sense) parking meter has received some research attention in the state of its origin; see LeRoy H. Fischer and Robert E. Smith, "Oklahoma and the Parking Meter," *Chronicles of Oklahoma*, XLVII, No. 2 (Summer, 1969), pp. 168-208.

Robert Venturi, in *Learning from Las Vegas . . .* (Rev. ed. Cambridge, Mass.: MIT Press, 1977), provides us with a contemporary model for understanding the commercial strip, while John Jakle and Richard L. Mattson, "The Evolution of a Commercial Strip," *Journal of Cultural Geography*, I, No. 2 (Summer, 1981), pp. 12-25, suggest a more historically oriented approach. Also useful in this context is Grady Clay's chapter on "The Strip" in his *Close-Up: How to Read the American City* (New York: Praeger, 1973), and three unpublished theses: Barry Gordon, "The Commercial Strip as an Indicator of American Cultural Themes" (M.A. thesis, Syracuse University, 1972), Louden C. Hoffman, "A Case Study of Commercial Strip Development: The Warsaw-Glenway Commercial Strip, Cincinnati, Ohio" (M.A. thesis, University of Cincinnati, 1968), and Robert F. Gould, "Strip Highway Settlement" (Ph.D. dissertation, University of Tennessee, 1969). Cultural commentators on the highway strip have multiplied like the strips themselves. One humorous and perceptive analyst has been Tom Wolfe, particularly in his *The Kandy-Kolored Tangerine-Flake Streamline Baby* (New York: Farrar, Straus & Giroux, 1965).

A group of road aficionados who have banded together in the Society for Commercial Archaeology (with organizational headquarters presently at the Library of the National Trust for Historic Preservation, 1785 Massachusetts Avenue, Washington, D.C., 20036) have also endeavored to treat the road as a cultural index. The group's range of interest is surveyed by Chester H. Liebs in an essay, "Remember Our Not-So-Distant Past?" *Historic Preservation*, XXX, No. 1 (Jan.-March, 1978), pp. 30-35. Commercial archaeologists are also beginning to establish a valuable literature that includes: Daniel Vieyra, *"Fill'er Up": An Architectural History of America's Gas Station* (New York: Macmillan, 1979); Richard J. S. Gutman and Elliott Kaufman, *American Diner* (New York: Harper & Row, 1979), and John Margolies, *The End of the Road: Vanishing Highway Architecture in America* (New York: Penguin Books, 1977). Each of these highly pictorial volumes should be read in concert with more systematic empirical studies such as those done by John Jakle on gasoline stations ("The American Gasoline Station, 1920 to 1970," *Journal of American Culture*, I, No. 3 [Fall, 1978], pp. 520-42) and on motels ("Motels By the Roadside: America's Room For The Night," *Journal of Cultural Geography*, I, No. 1 [Fall-Winter, 1980], pp. 34-49). Two other works on motels, our homes away from home when on the road, also have been very helpful to me: one, a short essay, "The Missing Motel," written by Reyner Benham almost two decades ago in *Landscape*, XV, No. 2 (Winter, 1965), pp. 4-6; the other, a recent book done by Warren J. Belasco, *Americans on the Road, From Autocamp to Motel, 1910-1945* (Cambridge, Mass.: MIT Press, 1979).

A Road Guide to U.S. 40 in Indiana, Past and Present

George Stewart's perceptive overview of *U.S. 40, Cross Section of the United States of America* (first published in 1953 by Houghton Mifflin, Boston, and reprinted in 1973 by Greenwood Press, Westport, Connecticut) is, unfortunately, all too brief in its treatment of U.S. 40 in Indiana. The National Road era of the route's history is, however, well documented. Lee Burns's earlier essay, *The National Road in Indiana* (Indiana Historical Society *Publications*, VII, No. 4, 1919), has been reprinted by the Public Library of Fort Wayne and Allen County in 1955. Also useful is a booklet, *Then and Now: The National Road and Its People*, edited by Patrick Steele and published in 1977 as part of an Indiana Committee for the Humanities grant project and sponsored by Historic Landmarks Foundation of Indiana and ICH. In addition to these local studies, information about the nineteenth-century history of U.S. 40 can be also found in surveys such as Robert Bruce, *The Old National Road* (Washington, D.C.: American Automobile Association, 1915) and Philip D. Jordan, *The National Road* (Indianapolis: Bobbs-Merrill, 1948).

More research, however, needs to be done on the U.S. 40 route as a nineteenth-century toll road and as a link in the National Old Trails Road Association in the early twentieth century. The latter is surveyed in two contemporary accounts: Charles Henry Davis, *The National Old Trails Road, Ocean to Ocean Highway* (Boston: Everett Press, 1914) and J. M. Lowe, *The National Old Trails Road* (Kansas City, Mo.: Published by the Author, 1924). Jane Fisher, wife of Carl Fisher, the Indiana businessman who promoted the Lincoln and Dixie highways, provides a familial portrait of her husband's road-developing career in *Fabulous Hoosier: A Story of American Achievement* (New York: R. M. McBride, 1947).

Issues of *The Hoosier Motorist* (1909-   ) afford the

researcher an excellent chronicle of the interaction of auto and highway during the U.S. 40 era, and David A. Ripple's four-volume, *History of the Interstate System in Indiana* (Lafayette, Ind.: Purdue University and the Indiana State Highway Commission, 1976) covers the period from the late 1930s through 1972. Ripple's work describes the development of both the national and state program, the evolution of policies and standards, route history, and the program's cost, funding, and general benefits. In this context I have also used, with profit, a publication of the U.S. Department of Transportation's Federal Highway Administration, *America's Highways, 1776-1976: A History of the Federal-Aid Program* (Washington, D.C.: U.S. Printing Office, 1976).

As is obvious to us all, the advent of the automobile changed forever the size, shape, and function of both the road and the roadscape. James Flink has been a masterful historian of this transformation, first in *America Adopts the Automobile, 1895-1910* (Cambridge, Mass.: MIT Press, 1970), and, later, in *The Car Culture* (Cambridge, Mass.: MIT Press, 1975). In this context, I would also recommend Cynthia Golomb Dettelbach, *In The Driver's Seat: The Automobile in American Literature and Popular Culture* (Westport, Conn.: Greenwood Press, 1976) and Ant Farm's *Automerica: A Trip Down U.S. Highways from World War II to the Future* (New York: E. P. Dutton, 1976).

For the concept of the "galactic city" emerging around America's interstate interchanges, I am indebted to Peirce Lewis's essay, "The Unprecedented City" in *The American Land* (Washington, D.C.: Smithsonian Exposition Books, 1979). For research on specific U.S. 40 communities and settlement patterns, I had the good fortune to read in the rich regional files being collected from across the state by the staff of the Indiana Guide project at the Indiana Historical Society. Learning more about individual communities required, in addition to examining their built environments closely, reading local studies such as George T. Blakey and Thomas Reed, *An Illustrated Guide To Historic Richmond* (n.d.) and Arthur Whallon, *Centerville, Indiana: A National Road Town* [1970], and Marjorie Hughes Walker (ed.), *A Glimpse of the Past of Hancock, Indiana* (1968). Two published interim reports done as part of the state's Historic Sites and Structures Inventory on *Wayne County* (1981) and *Putnam County* (1982) also widened my appreciation of both academic and vernacular architecture of those areas through which the U.S. route passes. *Indianapolis Architecture* (Indianapolis: Indiana Architectural Foundation, 1975), of course, is a must resource for any student of Washington Street's route through the city. Finally, two volumes of travel accounts by visitors to Indiana contained some description of their impressions along the U.S. 40 route; consult *Indiana as Seen By Early Travelers* (Indianapolis: Indiana Historical Bureau, 1916), edited by Harlow Lindley, and *Travel Accounts of Indiana, 1679-1961* (Indianapolis: Indiana Historical Bureau, 1970), edited by Shirley S. McCord.

Despite the enormous role that the production and distribution of mobile homes and manufactured housing plays in the contemporary Indiana economy, we have little scholarship on the subject. A statistical compendium by Carlton M. Edwards, *Homes for Travel and Living: The History and Development of the Recreational and Mobile Home Industries* (East Lansing, Mich.: Carl Edwards, 1977), is a useful reference work. Margaret J. Drury, *Mobile Homes: The Unrecognized Revolution in American Housing* (New York: Praeger, 1972) and Michael A. Rockland, *Homes on Wheels* (New Brunswick, N.J.: Rutgers University Press, 1980) are two succinct introductions to the topic.

Road workers are also a part of the American labor force still largely neglected by historians. Works that I have found useful include Jane Stern, *Trucker: A Portrait of the Last American Cowboy* (New York:

McGraw Hill, 1975), Clara Z. Keyton's *Tourist Camp Pioneering Experiences* (Chicago: Adams Press, 1960), and David Morton, "They Did It All for You," *Progressive Architecture*, VI, No. 18 (June, 1978), pp. 40-44. On one type of famous roadside advertisers, see Frank Rowsome, *The Verse by the Side of the Road: The Story of the Burma-Shave Signs and Jingles* (Brattleboro, Vt.: Stephen Greene Press, 1965), and for a series of playful vignettes of men and women whose lives and livelihoods often abut the highway, read William Least Heat Moon, *Blue Highways: A Journey into America* (Boston: Atlantic-Little Brown, 1983). A number of the "blue highways" (so marked on maps since they are two-lane roads at best) that Moon travels are rural, as is the U.S. 40 route for a large segment of its journey across Indiana. To help decipher the built-environment of such a landscape, I would strongly recommend a publication, *Minnesota Farmscape: Looking at Change*, prepared by the Minnesota Historical Society in 1980.

In order to attract would-be customers, roadside entrepreneurs have tried all types of architectural and environmental gimmicks. The student of the twentieth-century American highway can find examples of this zaniness in an eclectic assortment of publications: Jim Heimann and Rip Georges, *California Crazy: Roadside Vernacular Architecture* (San Francisco: Chronicle Books, 1980); Paul Hirshorn and Steven Izenour, *White Towers* (Cambridge, Mass.: MIT Press, 1979); *The World of Ronald McDonald*, edited by Marshall Fishwick (Bowling Green, Ohio: Popular Press, 1976); two books by Jane and Michael Stern, one on *Amazing America* (New York: Random House, 1977) and another, *Roadfood* (New York: Random House, 1978), plus the already mentioned *End of the Road* book by Margolies. For information on a road particularly important to many Hoosiers, see Al. Bloemker's *500 Miles to Go: The Story of the Indianapolis Speedway* (New York: Coward-McCann, 1961). Other important symbols are the state's county courthouses, several of which grace the U.S. 40 route, and all of which have been studied by David R. Hermansen in his essay, *Indiana County Courthouses of the Nineteenth Century* (Muncie, Ind.: Ball State University, 1968).